GOD
CALLED HER
ADAM

Emme Masters

To Courtney

May blessings explode
in your life now and until

Emme Masters

ISBN 978-1-64299-814-6 (paperback)
ISBN 978-1-64299-917-4 (hardcover)
ISBN 978-1-64299-815-3 (digital)

Christian Faith Publishing, Inc.
832 Park Avenue
Meadville, PA 16335
www.christianfaithpublishing.com

Cover design by Angela Freeman Lewis of AF Creative Source Designs, LLC

Printed in the United States of America

Dedication

To those who have bound or been bound by the
chains of the judgement against her; this book is
dedicated to your freedom found through Christ.

To my family who tirelessly supports my endeavors
and intentionally finds the good in them all;
this book acknowledges your loyalty.

To my husband, my Ish, my attention, affections and admiration
remain turned toward you. Your insistence that I continue
forward in times when I felt there was nothing left will always be
remembered. Your leadership, intelligence and valor are perpetual
beacons that I willingly pursue. Thank you for being as God
intended. This book acknowledges who I am in light of God's
plan when He presented me to you - your Isha, your Woman.

Contents

Introduction

This book is not for the faint of heart. We will dive into the Word and question all that is written and spoken. We will challenge our thoughts about what we have read and how we have perceived the rightful implications. You will examine your thinking.

For the content of this book to have full effect, you must commit to yourself to spend time with each thought. Look at each thought from every angle. This kind of examination is an intentionally slow process.

Thinking in this way will expose the areas where you have, inextricably, connected two (or more) thoughts that may not require connection. Sometimes we make these connections out of convenience, but sometimes we make these connections passively. It is the connections made passively—without intention or effort—that are of interest to us. These are the thoughts that can make subtle, incremental shifts in our thinking and lead us to erroneous or illogical conclusions.

Religion in general has been labeled by skeptics as an emotional crutch for the weak-minded; however, in my examination, Christianity is for the thinking person as well as all others. The tenants of the faith are reasonable, and the relationship with the Eternal God is satisfying beyond the expression of words.

This worldview is powerful and launches from reason into an atmosphere of faith always tethered to the one who is, the Word.

From the precipice of God's Word, this book reexamines the identity of women. Who was the first woman at creation? Who do we perceive her to be now? How are our ideas of women molded and expressed by women, men, children and society as a whole?

To help answer these questions, we will review the story of the creation of humanity. In doing so, this book will challenge what most

Christians have been taught. Using questions and answers in a workbook format, as well as short stories, expect to see God's Word come to life. If you are a woman, you can expect to see who you were intended to be versus who you were told to be, or even who you are. If you are not a woman, expect to be challenged to accept God's idea of who women should be versus the misshapen perception of women that has caused the unequal relationship between men and women throughout history and into the present era. Working through the ideas presented in this book will expose the consequences for all of us when women are forced into a mold that is too small for the expanse of the gift God has given them.

Venture into the thoughts presented on these pages. Make a habit of breaking unnecessary thought pairing. Slowly review each thought and do your best to test it to ensure it can stand on its own. Make the thought independent.

*****

For your convenience, I have included a key to the abbreviations used for Bible versions;

NASB - New American Standard Bible
KJV - King James Version
NKJV - New King James Version
YLT - Young's Literal Translation
HCSB - Holman Christian Study Bible
BSB - Berean Study Bible
ICB - International Children's Bible
MTB - Mechanical Translated Bible
ESV - English Standard Version

Dispersed throughout the book, I have included fictionalized narratives of the creation story. Each section is identified with text of "Imagine …" I hope you enjoy these words, these thoughts, this expression of the love of the One who made us and gave us all good things to enjoy.

Chapter 1

Foundation

The Bible ... describe it.

A repository for timeless ideas of right and wrong? A quaint book full of outdated ideas? Although we might never say it aloud, some of us think the Bible is full of antiquated notions of modesty and, sadly, irrelevant for our technologically advanced societies. Perhaps the Bible is better described as a book whose ideas could have been right in the time it was written or in some instances today but whose ideas of absolute right and wrong no longer apply.

Over time, the idea that the Bible had limited relevance to my everyday life became what I thought. These were some of the ideas that I accepted without thinking, but what if God really created us in His image? What if God created us for a purpose? What if God loves us?

Is it possible that a loving God would gift us a treasure of wisdom to make sure we find total satisfaction in this fallen world?

Yes, suppose God really loves you. Is it such a stretch to believe the ideas and philosophies put forth in the Bible keep you from harm and maximize your fun and pleasure?

What if the Bible is what it claims to be? What if it is a deeply insightful look into humanity authored by the Creator Himself? Imagine that, out of love, God gave us the Bible to expose our fragile inner workings so we can know how to protect ourselves from damage and hurt.

Let God show you, through the Bible, how He intended the first woman to change the world and the landscape of Adam's world. Discover how this created being was designed to ensure that Adam's life would never be the same while also satisfying her greatest dreams and aspirations. Finally, and astonishingly, absorb how a woman's God-gifted sexuality is an astonishing force deserving protection for *her* best life.

Basic Principles

If a swimmer stays underwater too long, should they be mocked for wanting to take a deep breath of air once their head crests the water? If a marathon runner practices in the summer sun, is their desire for a refreshing drink of water an idea who's time has past in light of our modern world? Think about our need to be loved by our parents. Is this need for love a primal instinct that modern humanity has eradicated for healthy development?

At times, it feels as though our natural inclinations go unanswered. Many times we find that our beliefs are actively invalidated by the people around us. Think about this.

Is the need to breath air, have a long drink of water or the love of your parents something humanity can or should move away from? Have these needs been modified through our participation in life classes, group counseling or a visit to the Christian living section at the local book store? Or are these needs deep and undeniable expressions of what is true? There is no question that these rich inner needs are expressions of who we are; to deny them is folly and leads to destruction.

The truth is, when you are submerged underwater for too long, you burn to take in fresh air.

The truth is, when you go for a brisk run in the noonday sun, you thirst for a deep drink of water.

The truth is, we all long to be loved by our parents.

This is *truth*.

Let's add another truth: God and His Word, the Holy Bible. When we deny God's instruction, we embark on a wide road away from His greatest plans for our lives.

The question is, do you accept this truth? If not, what do you believe? What is your foundation?

What if God loved you so much He wrote down how you could avoid everything that comes to make your life *less*?

Let's take a moment to think this through and start at the beginning.

So, tell me ...

Who Are You?

Let's establish a few things first. This book was written for those who subscribe to or wish to subscribe to the Christian worldview. To see if you fall into this category, answer the following questions:

1. Do you believe in God?
2. Do you believe Jesus died for your sins, and then came back to life and sits with His Father in heaven?
3. Do you accept Jesus as your Lord?
   If you answered yes to these questions, you are a Christian.

4. Are you a Christian?

Many people describe themselves as Christian but it is one thing to say you are a Christian—a little Christ—and quite another to *be* a little Christ. When you consider your words and behavior, do they express Christian beliefs? If you knew someone who speaks like you speak, who valued what you value and who acts the way you act, would you think he or she was a Christian? Think deeply to answer these questions and then take your time answering questions 5 and 6.

5. What does being a Christian look like in your life?
6. What does being a Christian look like in the lives of your Christian friends?

We do not typically ask these self-probing questions. We tend to live without reflecting on what we actually believe. This lack of self-assessment can allow us to adopt ideas that would be excluded immediately if we made a habit of inspecting ideas or, as the Bible calls it, guarding our hearts.

Younger people should be especially careful to guard their hearts. This means not letting ideas or images passively into your heart and mind but to thoughtfully consider these ideas before accepting or rejecting them. It can be a difficult task, but it must become a habit.

On the internet, it is easy to be accidentally exposed to images or situations you should never see or hear, so be careful. Guard yourself. Guard your heart!

We need to make sure we still believe the ideas we want to believe and that we still reject those things we should not believe. We need to make sure we make rational and biblical sense. This means living according to an immovable standard—Jesus.

Each week, do a quick assessment. Ask yourself the preceding questions but also ask the following questions.

7. Do you read the Bible without being prompted?
    • How often?
    • If not, why?

8. How does the Bible affect your life?
9. What is your favorite theme of the Bible?
    • Why?

Who Do You Think God Is?

If I speak a word to you, an image will come into your mind. This is the way we are wired.

So, do this exercise with me.

Think of God as if He is physically with you right now. With this in mind, answer the next questions. With this in mind, answer the next questions.

10. What is the first image that comes to mind?

Write down or draw the image that you see when I say "God."

11. Describe the characteristics of this image.
    What is the expression on His face? Is He looking at you?

Review your answers to the last two questions. This will reveal a lot about your inner image of God.

The next questions are for those who saw God with a less-than-pleasant expression on His face.

1. Is God angry with you?
2. How does God express His love for you?

List the ways God expresses His love for you in every-day life.

Now we are getting to the roots of your foundation.

God is love. (1 Jn 4:8b, NASB)

Reflect on the last few questions about your image of God and His expression of love for you.

God is love and He is also our Father. Not a dysfunctional, distant father but a father who lavishes love on His children. Holy Scripture says God is our "Abba," our Daddy. Think on this for a moment. God is not a father who requires us to do everything correctly and in a timely manner for Him to love us. God is a Father who desires to be active in the lives of those He loves. He is always available and He provides us with wisdom and other good gifts. These verses are a small sample of the numerous Scriptures telling us that God is our loving father.

For you did not receive a spirit that makes you a slave again to fear, but you received the Spirit of sonship. And by him we cry, 'Abba, Father.' (Rom 8:15, NASB)

"And I will be a father to you, and you shall be sons and daughters to Me," says the Lord Almighty." (2 Cor 6:18, NASB)

Praise the God and Father of our Lord Jesus Christ, who has blessed us in Christ with every spiritual blessing in the heavens. 4 For He chose us in Him, before the foundation of the world, to be holy and blameless in His sight. In love 5 He predestined us to be adopted through Jesus Christ for Himself, according to His favor and will (Eph 1:3–5, HCSB)

Now, prepare to think deeply about the following questions.

1. Do you believe the Bible is true?
2. What is your biggest stumbling block within the Bible?
3. If I looked at your life, would I be able to determine you believed the Bible is true? How?

The answers to these questions are very important. They are the foundation on which you build your life.

Confidence is the natural expression of faith.

Confidence = a belief, idea or construct x faith

Which of your beliefs exude confidence? Do you have confidence in the basic principles of your faith? Where have you placed your confidence?

If you believe the Bible is true, you will consider what the Bible says when you live your life. You will try not to lie, think more highly of yourself, or take advantage of other people. Why? Because the Bible says these and other such behaviors are wrong.

Do you believe the Bible? If so, what does the Bible say about worshipping other gods? What does it say about respecting or obeying authority? How does the Bible say you should conduct yourself in marriage?

If you don't know the answer to these questions, that is precisely the point. Many people say they believe the Bible is true but they don't know what the Bible *says*. So, while these people may *want* to believe the Bible is true, they don't actually believe it because they don't know what is written in its pages.

Suppose you were asked, 'Do you believe everything in this book?'

You could say 'Yes, I believe everything in this book.' So, think about this. You probably are reading this book from front to back. You are now in the first few pages. It is not possible for you to believe everything in this book because you don't know what is *in* this book.

You may trust my integrity as an author that I would not intentionally tell you anything inaccurate; however, you don't yet know what I intend to tell you. Get it?

The other option is to say, 'No, I don't believe everything in this book.' This would likely be accurate, although again, you don't have enough information to *know* this.

That said, make a habit to *always* find something in everything you read, outside of Scripture, that you don't agree with. It keeps your mind sharp and creates a habit in you that prevents you from mindlessly letting someone else's ideas shape you.

If you think I'm saying that unless you read the *entire* Bible you can't say you believe everything in it, you are correct. But you may have set your mind to be ready to accept the ideas you see in the Bible as you discover them. This is the best start.

Staying with this idea of using the Bible as a foundation of truth, dig into what is says about a very relevant topic in our world today: the identity of women and their differences from men.

An easy subject to think about, in this regard, especially in our world today, is sex.

1. What does God say about sex?
2. What does He say about sex inside marriage?
3. What does He say about sex outside marriage?

4. Why does God make this distinction?
5. Are the rules about sexual relationships the same for men and women?

These questions force you to examine your thoughts about God, sex, the Bible, and your life.

Take a moment to think about your answers to these questions. If I asked these same questions to you ten minutes from now, giving you time to consider the accuracy of your answers, would your responses be the same? More detailed? Would you notice you may need to spend more time with God's Word? Do you see how much of your view of the Bible is shaped *outside* of the Bible?

One more set of questions to round out this chapter.

1. Are men and women the same
    a) Physically?
    b) Emotionally?
    c) Spiritually?

Keep your answers in mind. We will devote much of this book to discussion of these responses.

In the Beginning

If we are to spend time trying to understand what God intended for humanity from the beginning of creation, we need to review the portion of the Bible that describes creation.

According to Genesis 1, humanity was created on day six of creation. The verses that recount this event are provided below:

> 26 Then God said, "Let Us make man in Our image, according to Our likeness. They will rule the fish of the sea, the birds of the sky, the livestock, all the earth, and the creatures that crawl on the earth."

27 So God created man in His own image;
He created him in the image of God; He created
them male and female.

28 God blessed them, and God said to
them, "Be fruitful, multiply, fill the earth, and
subdue it. Rule the fish of the sea, the birds of
the sky, and every creature that crawls[j] on the
earth." God also said, "Look, I have given you
every seed-bearing plant on the surface of the
entire earth and every tree whose fruit contains
seed. This food will be for you, 30 for all the
wildlife of the earth, for every bird of the sky,
and for every creature that crawls on the earth—
everything having the breath of life in it. I have
given every green plant for food." And it was so.
31 God saw all that He had made, and it was very
good. Evening came and then morning: the sixth
day. (Gen. 1:26–31, HCSB)

An additional detail regarding the creation of humanity is
located in Genesis 5:2.

2 Male and female created he them; and
blessed them, and called their name Adam, in
the day when they were created. (Gen. 5:2, KJV)

What do you think of the fact that God called both male and
female "Adam?"

If this fact disturbs or unsettles you, you should work to identify the cause.

When God called both male and female Adam, it implies God
sees them as equal. Perhaps, you remember from your childhood
Sunday school lessons that Woman was always called Eve and you
need a minute in ingest this additional information. Could this be
the source of your discomfort? In any case, we will spend some time
studying this verse.

Take a moment to determine if any of your beliefs are injured if God made no distinction between male and female by name.

For those I met while researching this book, a few ideas were brought up repeatedly in refutation of this verse. For example, some translations of the Bible use the word *humanity* instead of *Adam*. Let me show you several translations of Genesis 5:2:

> He created them male and female. When they were created, He blessed them and called them man. (HCSB)
> He created them male and female, and He blessed them and named them Man in the day when they were created. (NASB)
> He created them male and female and blessed them. And he named them "Mankind" when they were created. (NIV)
> He created them male and female, and blessed them and called them Mankind in the day they were created. (NKJV)
> a male and a female He hath prepared them, and He blesseth them, and calleth their name Man, in the day of their being prepared. (YLT)

These translations use a different word for Adam, but as a testament to their integrity, the NASB, NIV, and HCSB translations make a clear note that the authentic word is not *humanity*, *man*, or *mankind* but *Adam*.

Maybe you agree with Scripture that God called them Adam, but there are some who have argued that Adam can be accurately translated to mean humanity or man in general as well as to mean the name of a person. This is true. The word *Adam* is found over five hundred times in the Old Testament. The vast majority of those times, over four hundred times, it is translated as *man* rather than as *Adam*, a proper noun. Adam is translated only thirteen times as a proper name, the name of a person.

With this revelation, you may think this could be a valid point for the translation of Genesis 5:2 but I request that you continue to read further. As you read, evaluate if your passion for the defense of the translation of Adam to a general term of man is based on anything other than the quest for truth. Be mindful to identify any cultural bias you may have ingested without thought. The discomfort, if any, could simply be a hesitancy to change a long-held belief based on the childhood stories about creation.

Genesis chapter 5 is a genealogy, a historical record of relationships of parents to children over generations. As such, we expect to see the name of the parent and then the name of the progeny. This is what is shown, in context, in this chapter. Please see the following excerpt from Genesis 5:

> This is the book of the generations of Adam. In the day that God created man, in the likeness of God made he him;
>
> 2 Male and female created he them; and blessed them, and called their name Adam, in the day when they were created.
>
> 3 And Adam lived an hundred and thirty years, and begat a son in his own likeness, and after his image; and called his name Seth:
>
> 4 And the days of Adam after he had begotten Seth were eight hundred years: and he begat sons and daughters:
>
> 5 And all the days that Adam lived were nine hundred and thirty years: and he died.
>
> 6 And Seth lived an hundred and five years, and begat Enos:
>
> 7 And Seth lived after he begat Enos eight hundred and seven years, and begat sons and daughters. (Gen 5:1–7, KJV)

Verses 1 and 2 begin with the name of both Adams. Verse 3 begins the lineage from the male Adam and records the genealogy through the fathers. This continues for the entirety of the chapter.

Given the pattern of name of parent, name of child, it should follow logically that the use of the word *Adam*, as a name, is the most rational conclusion.

The second argument against believing the word *Adam* is the name of both the male and the female states that because the single name is given to two genders, God could not have meant Adam as a proper noun; a name. Instead, those who follow this thought think God is required to use unique names or perhaps this is another instance of the translators using their discretion.

To help sort this out, I have provided the Hebrew text of Genesis 5:1–3 from the Masoretic text:

זֶה סֵפֶר תּוֹלְדֹת אָדָם בְּיוֹם בְּרֹא אֱלֹהִים אָדָם בִּדְמוּת
אֱלֹהִים עָשָׂה אֹתוֹ:
זָכָר וּנְקֵבָה בְּרָאָם וַיְבָרֶךְ אֹתָם וַיִּקְרָא אֶת־שְׁמָם אָדָם
בְּיוֹם הִבָּרְאָם: ס
וַיְחִי אָדָם שְׁלֹשִׁים וּמְאַת שָׁנָה וַיּוֹלֶד בִּדְמוּתוֹ כְּצַלְמוֹ
וַיִּקְרָא אֶת־שְׁמוֹ שֵׁת:

The Hebrew spelling of Adam is אָדָם. Review the Hebrew text to find the word *Adam*. The Hebrew word for 'Adam' is in **bold** font for you:

זֶה סֵפֶר תּוֹלְדֹת **אָדָם** בְּיוֹם בְּרֹא אֱלֹהִים אָדָם בִּדְמוּת
אֱלֹהִים עָשָׂה אֹתוֹ:
אָדָם זָכָר וּנְקֵבָה בְּרָאָם וַיְבָרֶךְ אֹתָם וַיִּקְרָא אֶת־שְׁמָם
בְּיוֹם הִבָּרְאָם: ס
וַיְחִי **אָדָם** שְׁלֹשִׁים וּמְאַת שָׁנָה וַיּוֹלֶד בִּדְמוּתוֹ וַיִּצְלְמוֹ
וַיִּקְרָא אֶת־שְׁמוֹ שֵׁת:

Now, compare the Hebrew to the NKJV of Genesis 5:1–3. The Hebrew word for 'Adam' is italicized for emphasis:

This is the book of the generations of *Adam*. In the day that God created man, in the likeness of God made he him;

2 Male and female created he them; and blessed them, and called their name *Adam*, in the day when they were created.

3 And *Adam* lived an hundred and thirty years, and begat a son in his own likeness, and after his image; and called his name Seth:

Now, compare the Hebrew to the NASB translation of Genesis 5:1–3:

This is the book of the generations of *Adam*. In the day when God created man, He made him in the likeness of God. He created them male and female, and He blessed them and named them *Man* in the day when they were created.

3 When *Adam* had lived one hundred and thirty years, he [*b*]became the father of a son in his own likeness, according to his image, and named him Seth

It is my contention that the word 'Adam' should be translated as 'Adam', a proper noun, in the context of this genealogy. If this is true, then in Genesis 5:2, it is also true that God called both male and female Adam.

Because both male and female were called Adam, I will refer to the female Adam as "*she*", "*her*" or the "other Adam."

In later chapters, we will discuss some of the implications of her existence during the time between her creation and her introduction to Adam.

With the creation story fresh in our minds, it is time to begin our trek into the truth of the Scriptures. Let's begin to study the details to understand the importance of God's creation of humanity.

Using fictionalized short stories based on Scripture, we will ensure our foundation is rooted firmly in what we discover to be the truth. Minimally, you will have an opportunity to identify if your basic beliefs and understandings are aligned with Scripture.

In the following narrative, you will have a chance to discover *her*. We will share in the delight of the creation of the second being in humanity.

And now, without further ado and in the light of God's love, I introduce to you, the other Adam ...

Imagine ...

Adam

With love as His eyes, God looked at Adam, who was breathing deeply while fast asleep resting on his side. Adam had fallen into a deep sleep, his arm lying loosely on his side. His hand, having fallen forward, left the back of his fingers caressing the stalks of grass, each breath causing his hand to move slightly back and forth.

God was very pleased with the creation of Adam. He was powerful, intelligent, daring, and … charming. "Well, *sometimes* charming," the Holy Spirit reminded God. They all laughed.

God returned to the sleeping man and knelt beside him deciding which bones to use to craft His next creation. No matter which bones He chose, Adam would not be harmed. After all, God was the surgeon.

Reaching forward, God parted Adam's exposed skin and removed a side. Carefully, as if hiding a secret, He closed the flesh back into place. God made a final check on Adam to ensure he was resting peacefully. God wanted him to sleep while his bones regenerated. Adam was going to be a bit sore when he woke.

God closed his hand over the portion He'd removed from Adam. Cradling it as He rose to His feet, God turned and walked to a distant clearing in another part of the garden.

Once the Father was settled in the place for the next creation, He set to work. He already had a vision of her. She would be full and curvy and slightly smaller than Adam in stature on the outside, but she would be amazingly powerful inside. Because He was crafting a human to be the functional opposite of Adam, her body would be the basket of life. She had to be *strong,* consistent. She had to be thoughtful.

God chuckled under His breath. "Yes, she is his opposite," He said with a twinkle in His eye.

God knew just how to join male and female both spiritually and physically. Both would find love for one another.

Kneeling once again, God bent over the earth and opened His hand to expose the bones He had just taken from Adam. Beginning with his free hand, the Father started shaping and bending this new

creature into being. With both hands at work, His vision was being revealed.

His touch alone commanded life to move through her, causing cells to multiply and organs to form. Like Adam, God made her in His image. Of course, she already possessed God's Spirit. She had been created from the creature made equally in the image of God and imbued with that same spirit.

In the same way God attended to every atom of detail in man, He attended to all things with her. And, in the same way God had called man Adam, God called his latest creation the same, Adam.

He sat back on his heels as He watched the final layer of skin thicken and complete. Lastly, the layer of life-giving fat fluffed out her cheeks, breasts, hips, and thighs in a way that would delight them both.

God watched her, checking once again to ensure she was all that she needed to be.

Oh, what a magnificent creation she was.

Looking at her, God noticed He was holding His breath.

God smiled as He exhaled. He loved her. As God's love poured from His hands into her being, she inhaled deeply, and her eyes started to flutter to life.

God removed his hands and shifted forward. He was kneeling again and bent His head forward to allow her to see His face once she opened her eyes.

God quickly dipped His head a bit to whisper into her ear.

"Adam. Daughter." God whispered and returned His face to just above hers.

Her eyes fluttered once more and then opened.

"Adam," God whispered again, "you are loved."

She exhaled …

Chapter 2

Purpose

Inside each human soul is a longing for purpose. It is not often that we can accurately use the word *each* or *every* with regard to humanity. The longing for purpose is one of these rare occasions.

Numerous categories of negative behavior are attributed to a lack of purpose but why do we have such a yearning for purpose? Why does our self-worth hinge on purpose? Does God intend your life to have purpose?

Again, we return to Scripture to find the answers that God has provided to His children.

> Then the Lord God took the man and put him into the Garden of Eden to cultivate it and keep it. (Gen 2:15, ICB)
>
> Then the Lord God said, "It is not good for the man to be alone. I will make a helper who is right for him." (Gen 2:18, ICB)

Humanity and God's Purpose

Adam had a purpose. Review Genesis 2:15. You may not think cultivating the garden was much of a purpose, but it was a God-given purpose, and it took full advantage of Adam's physical and intellectual talents. This purpose challenged Adam's creative powers, his planning and his forethought. Cultivation of the garden, or "work," would allow God to bless the work of Adam's hands. Eden also provided the perfect opportunity for scientific discovery.

But what of the other Adam? Where was her purpose? Did she even have one?

Yes!

Whereas Adam was created and then given a purpose, *her* purpose was announced prior to her creation.

Review Genesis 2:18.

If your reaction is anything like mine, this scriptural truth gives you no deep satisfaction. *None.*

Adam was given to agriculture. Was *she* a domestic? It doesn't seem right. Not that being a domestic is bad but if there are only two people, millions of acres available and every opportunity abounded, how could it be right that she was to serve him?

Don't laugh. This notion of the woman's role in relationships and to the world is one reason so many women reject Christianity.

To this end, a great deal of effort is being put forth to "instruct young women" in how to be good helpers to their mates - ensuring modern women serve their Adam. Unfortunately, this misguided idea of help has perverted a noble effort and diverted the time, talents and energy of many of the daughters of God.

We need to read and understand the Bible, God's love letter to us, because by reading His word, we see the Father's heart for women.

God made women to be a "help," not a "helper."

Let's discuss this important distinction by looking at various translations of Genesis 2:18.

> And the Lord God said, "It is not good that the man should be alone; I will make him an help meet for him." (KJV)
>
> Then the Lord God said, "It is not good for the man to be alone; I will make him a helper suitable for him." (NASB)

Then the Lord God said, "It is not good that the man should be alone; I will make him a helper fit for him." (ESV)

Then the Lord God said, "It is not good for the man to be alone. I will make a helper as his complement." (HCSB)

Then the Lord God said, "It is not good for the man to be alone. I will make a helper who is right for him." (ICB)

Later, the Lord God said, "It is not good for the man to be alone. I will make the woman to be an authority corresponding to him." (ISB)

And Yhwh the Elohiym said, it is not functional for the human to exist by himself, I will make for him a helper as his opposite, (MTB)

And Jehovah God saith, 'Not good for the man to be alone, I do make to him an helper—as his counterpart.' (YLT)

Take a moment to review the many ways this verse is translated. Each translation, although slightly different, is faithful to convey a similar meaning.

Let's hone in on what the King James Version calls a "help meet." When thinking of a help meet, what do you envision? A helper? Those of us with a purely Christian background tend to think of someone (a woman) who meets the need of another (a man). In the case of the creation story, it would be the *her* meeting the needs of Adam.

Spoiler Alert: This book does not seek to contradict the picture that this other Adam was created to fulfil God's plan and to create a better environment for the man and their descendants. This book will, however, challenge you to think about what those needs were and how fulfilment of God's purpose for *her* crafted how men and women relate to each other. This book seeks to help you understand what it takes to be a "help meet," how incredible God's daughters are and were created to be … from the beginning.

Ezer: Help, Helper, Help Meet

The Hebrew word *ezer* is translated as "help, helper, help meet" in many popular English Bible translations. Generally, readers don't take the time to look up the definition of a word for which they already have a well-established meaning. This habit is why I, and I suspect you, didn't take the next step of dissecting the word. We almost missed a treasure hidden in plain sight.

A quick internet search reveals that "ezer" is used twenty-one times in the Old Testament. Of the twenty-one times this word is found in the Old Testament; eighteen of these mentions refer to the Lord; two directly refer to the "other Adam" in Genesis and the word is used once in Ezekiel to describe soldiers "...those who help him."

Read the following verses taken from the NASB translation, aloud. While you are reading, recognize that when you say the word "help", you are speaking about the characteristics God placed inside His *ezer*.

> And this regarding Judah; so he said, "Hear, O Lord, the voice of Judah, And bring him to his people. With his hands he contended for them, And may You be a help [ezer] against his adversaries." (Deut 33:7)
>
> "There is none like the God of Jeshurun, Who rides the heavens to your help [ezer], And through the skies in His majesty. (Deut 33:26)
>
> "Blessed are you, O Israel; Who is like you, a people saved by the Lord, Who is the shield of your help [ezer] And the sword of your majesty! So your enemies will cringe before you, And you will tread upon their high places." (Deut 33.29)
>
> The other was named Eliezer, for he said, "The God of my father was my help [ezer], and delivered me from the sword of Pharaoh." (Ex 18:4)

May He send you help [ezer] from the sanctuary and support you from Zion! (Ps 20:2)

Our soul waits for the Lord; He is our help [ezer] and our shield. (Ps 33:20)

But I am afflicted and needy; Hasten to me, O God! You are my help [ezer] and my deliverer; O Lord, do not delay. (Ps 70:5)

Once You spoke in vision to Your godly ones, and said, "I have given help [ezer] to one who is mighty; I have exalted one chosen from the people. (Ps 89:19)

O Israel, trust in the Lord; He is their help [ezer] and their shield. 10 O house of Aaron, trust in the Lord; He is their help [ezer] and their shield. 11 You who fear the Lord, trust in the Lord; He is their help [ezer] and their shield. (Ps 115:9–11)

I will lift up my eyes to the mountains; From where shall my help [ezer] come? 2 My help [ezer] comes from the Lord, Who made heaven and earth. (Ps 121:1–2)

Our help [ezer] is in the name of the Lord, Who made heaven and earth. (Ps 124:8)

How blessed is he whose help [ezer] is the God of Jacob, Whose hope is in the Lord his God. (Ps 146:5)

"Everyone will be ashamed because of a people who cannot profit them, who are not for help [ezer] or profit, but for shame and also for reproach. (Is 30:5)

"I will scatter to every wind all who are around him, his help [ezer] and all his troops; and I will draw out a sword after them. (Ez 12:14)

"Now when they fall they will be granted a little help [ezer], and many will join with them in hypocrisy. (Dan 11:34)

It is your destruction, O Israel, that you are
against Me, against your help [ezer]. (Hos 13:9)

Now that you have the facts of the *pure* meaning of *ezer*, do you still think women were created to be servants?

Psalms. 146:5 says, "How blessed is he whose help is the God of Jacob."

Let's restate this using what we have learned:

"How blessed is Adam, whose help is *her*."

Think on this.

This substitution of *her* for *ezer* is an effort to highlight the enormous charge that was given to her. In no way is this book attempting to say that *she* was the "God of Jacob." God is God. There is no other. However, *she* was blatantly, gifted by God to "help."

What is undeniably being broadcast here is this: as the God of Jacob was a "help," God equipped Woman to be an invaluable partner. She was a reservoir of talent and ideas, strength and encouragement, protection and a source of comfort for him, for herself, for her family and for humanity.

Exodus 18:4 says, "the God of my father was my *ezer*."

Think long and deep about this.

Scripture is shouting that *she* was intended to help Adam but not in any likeness to the servant that we train our Christian daughters to be.

Let's continue in our journey to reveal *her*.

୧ᆓ⊙ A Peek Inside Her

The word "ezer" is translated as "help." To translate this word as help is like choosing to use the word "cat" when you are intending to convey a lion.

A few Hebrew words are essential when working to reveal God's clearly prescribed plan. To understand these words in context, we need to have a rudimentary lesson in Hebrew.

Hebrew is one of a small number of languages read from right to left. In Hebrew script, each letter has a meaning. By examining the meaning of the letters, you will see how letters form word pictures. Because of this brilliant language construction, Hebrew words can communicate many layers of meaning. By understanding the meaning of the letters in a word and the order of the letters in the word, we will gain a deeper and more accurate meaning of the word as a whole.

To keep this idea simple, we will examine only the words of interest to this discussion but challenge yourself to explore Hebrew further after finishing this book.

Look at this word "*ezer*" written in Hebrew: עֵזֶר The letters are *ayin* (ע), *zayin* (ז) and *reysh* (ר).

This word is shown in modern Hebrew; however, the letters in the Hebrew language have changed over the thousands of years this language has existed.

The word *ezer* written in Ancient Hebrew with Moses' hand looked like this: ୧ᆓ⊙

Ayin began as a drawing of an eye. *Zayin* began as a drawing of a cutting tool or weapon. *Reysh* began as a drawing of a person's head.

As a quick exercise, think of what these symbols could mean.

ayin ⊙ to see; to know

zayin ᆓ to cut; to cut off

reysh ୧ the chief; the head; a person

As mentioned before, Hebrew can have layered meanings, so now that we know the meanings of each letter, let's resume study of this word.

This three-letter word can be studied many ways:

- o The first and second letters + the third letter
- o The first letter + the second and third letters
- o A single word

The first and second letters + the third letter – ℚ + ℐ ◉

ℐ◉ to know a weapon. This word is translated as "strong."
ℚ the chief; the head; a person

We see that an *ezer* is a strong person or strong one.
The first letter + the second and third letters – ℚ ℐ + ◉

◉ to see; to know
ℚℐ to cut off the person or head. This word is translated as "enemy."

We see that an *ezer* has the ability to see or identify the enemy.

With this simple exercise, we have discovered two characteristics of an *ezer*. She was created to be a strong person who has the ability to identify the enemy.

Does it surprise you to know that these traits are the components of the God-created woman? Can you see how these talents would be an advantage for all who encountered her?

We have only begun to explore who *she* really is.

Kenegedo (Neged)

When God mentions a "suitable help meet," He says an *ezer kenegedo*. In the last section, we studied what God means by *ezer*. What does God intend for us to understand by *ezer kenegedo*?

Kenegedo is a Hebrew word that means suitable, functional, or opposite, like a complement.

Whenever God is thinking of creating the other Adam, He says—both times—that He will make an *ezer kenegedo*. God says He will make a strong, insightful person who is the functional, suitable or opposite of Adam.

What does *kenegedo* mean in Hebrew?

Let's take this step by step:

- Functional—God gives the command to be fruitful. God gives this command to Adam after He creates the other Adam. This is logical. Before *she* was created, Adam could not be fruitful and multiply. She is functional meaning *she* enables them to procreate.
- Suitable—Because God is the giver of good gifts, we can be assured that the second created being was a complement to Adam. She is not a complement to mean *she* "completes" him. Rather, their temperaments and personalities fit well together.
- Opposite—This idea ties in neatly with "functional." Think of what it means to be opposite. Newton's third law of physics states that for every action there is an equal and opposite reaction. To be wholly opposite, one must be equal.

This other Adam was the equal creation to the initial Adam, although she had vastly different perspectives, gifts and talents.

Take a moment to consider the information we have just uncovered. Do you believe it? If you have only just begun to believe this, how will it cause you to live differently?

What Does It Take?

List ten traits the Lord exhibits when He is our help, our *ezer*. I will start you off with one and you compile the next nine.

1. Compassion
2. _____
3. _____
4. _____
5. _____
6. _____
7. _____
8. _____
9. _____
10. _____

Now list ten traits that *she* would have had to be imbued with to be Adam's help, his *ezer*. Once again, I will start you off with one and you can compile the next nine.

1. Strength
2. _____
3. _____
4. _____
5. _____
6. _____
7. _____
8. _____
9. _____
10. _____

Review both lists.

Most of the ten traits were the same and both were very impressive.

The idea that the Lord and the ezer share many traits is something you need to drink in slowly. Take time to let it sink in. If you go too quickly, it could be like water being splashed onto parched ground. It won't absorb but will merely run off. You might miss a wonderful opportunity to recognize who you really are.

Only after the ground has been softened can it absorb life-giving moisture. Let the fertile ground of your mind soften to accept this biblical truth.

Now for the final exercise for this chapter.

Just For Her ...

Choose five of the ten traits you named for the other Adam. For each of these traits, describe three jobs or careers that benefit from this trait. I have done the first one for you.

1. Strength
   a) Military
   b) Construction
   c) Engineering
2. _____
   a) _____
   b) _____
   c) _____
3. _____
   a) _____
   b) _____
   c) _____
4. _____
   a) _____
   b) _____
   c) _____
5. _____
   a) _____
   b) _____
   c) _____

Conclusion

If you completed these exercises, I trust you have a newfound appreciation for who God created women to be.

Always remember what you have discovered. This is a discovery about you, if you are a woman, and about your daughters, sisters, mother or wife.

Keep these ideas close as you continue to read the rest of this book.

God loves women. God empowered women. God has given biblical instruction to protect his most precious women.

And now, let's return to the place of God's creation of the other Adam ...

The Other Adam

Hhhhhhhhhhhhhhhhhhhhhhhhhhhhhhhhhh …

She exhaled slowly unaware that she had ever inhaled. Her lungs released the air placed there by the love of God.

She finished her first breath. Her eyes opened and adjusted to a radiant glory. The first image to greet them was the face of God. God looked deeply into her eyes as she searched His face. Feeling the love God had spoken of but a breath ago, she felt peace surrounding her like a soft blanket. She reached out for Him and He obliged by helping her into a sitting position.

She turned her head slowly as she took in her surroundings. The lush, rich greenery. The sparkling darkness of the earth. The brilliant colors of the sky. And then the Father … there was the Father.

An indescribable being who, though He looked like her, was not like her at all. But He … loved her.

At first, words were difficult in coming but, as she gathered her thoughts, they became a lazy stream of baskets to convey her thoughts. Eventually, the stream became an ocean out of which she drank and plundered as her gift of communication unfurled to its near full length.

Captivated by the expanse and the filling of her mind, she looked up when she heard God speaking in the distance. He was right before her so she trained her attention on Him knowing that His words were important.

She listened to God's magnificent stories. Although He looked to be her state (later she would say age), her spirit told her He was much deeper than she was or would ever be. Somehow, she knew He held indescribable wisdom and power.

God stood and walked slowly around the clearing. Looking in her direction, He winked and smiled. She heard Him say something but she couldn't quite make it out.

The ground was dark and rich but not hard. It looked as though it had been tilled but it hadn't been. Sprigs of grass popped from the ground randomly as seeds made their way to maturity.

41

Adam, as she was called, took it all in. She rose and followed Him closely. Listening intently as He spoke in what, at times, seemed like a whisper.

Suddenly, He paused and looked up. Holding out His hand, palm down, He invited a massive insect to land there. It fluttered its wings gracefully for balance as it touched each of its tiny legs onto the landing place.

Swinging around rather suddenly and bringing His hand and face near her, God said, "Daughter, what would you call this creature?"

A feeling she couldn't describe welled up in her and she felt as though she would explode. Joy and excitement poured out of her as if she was a container way too small for this abundance.

She brought her hands up to the delicate creature and, with eye lashes nearly brushing the design in the wings, she looked up, stepped back and declared.

"This creature is a beautifly. It is beautiful, and it flies."

She looked up at him, her eyes peering from under a storm of curly hair and smiled.

God looked at her once again, taking her in with His eyes. He loved her more than she could know. Yet, He was sure she knew as much as she could know the purity and intensity of His love.

He was already enjoying what He had planned for her for the rest of that day. He would ensure she had a good end.

Rejoining the moment with her, God said, "This beautifully marked creature is called butterfly."

He wiggled His fingers gently and the winged marvel's tiny legs lifted and moved away as its wings pushed against the air.

God settled back onto His haunches. Using His finger to draw a map of the garden in the dirt, He circled places He wanted her to discover and share with the man whom she would meet before the day ended.

She stood behind God. She had draped herself forward, her torso resting against His back. After some doing, she settled into a comfortable arrangement, resting her elbows on one of His wide shoulders, her hands cradling her head, one hand on each cheek.

Jesus and the Holy Spirit were taken in by the transparency of her pleasure of being in Their presence.

She watched in silence as God finished making circles on the map. He turned his head slightly to look at her.

"Adam," He said gently, catching her attention as she realized she had been looking at her arms and fingers admiring the delicateness in which she had been crafted.

Hearing God call to her, she looked up. With her attention back on Him, God continued. "I need you to go to this place, examine what is there and report back to me." He pointed to one of the circles on the map in the far corner of the garden.

She sprang to her feet. "Yes, Abba (Daddy). When would you like me to travel there?" She moved to get a better look at the map.

God was still settled near the ground. "You may go now if you like."

"I would *love* to go." She beamed as she, once again, felt her sense of discovery rising. "Are you coming with me?" *she* asked, not out of fear but out of a longing to never be outside of her Abba's presence.

"Yes, daughter. Nothing can separate you from My love."

Smiling, *she* stared down at the map God had drawn in the soil, memorizing the path to her destination. As she took off in that direction, she grabbed God's hand and, being assured of His presence, made her way to the outer part of Eden.

Somewhere along the journey, the Father's hand transformed from a physical one to a full spiritual presence. His state of being meant nothing to her because His presence was all around her.

It took many steps to reach the outer parts of the garden. When she arrived, her feet were laden with the dark earth. She dragged her feet slowly to wipe the clumps of earth from her feet.

Uneven dark patches of dirt dotted the ground creating a trail behind her like breadcrumbs marking the way back.

She had been excited before, but now she was transfixed by the overwhelming sights and sounds of activity and the beauty of that place. God was a giver of good gifts. Everything around was alive! A buzzing sound zipped past her ear.

"Bee!" she yelled to no one in particular.

An animal with long arms and sad eyes swung down from a nearby tree. It waddled toward her using its arms to propel itself forward in a loping manner. She was sure it was one of the creatures God wanted her to remember. She made a mental note.

She laughed out loud at her own observation. What next? Her mind moved at a dizzying speed. She alternated between sweeping observations to meticulously detailed attention on items of interest. She was enjoying the sights, smells and sounds of this maelstrom of exquisiteness.

She spun in excitement, falling down in delight. As she lay there laughing and squinting against the late afternoon sun, she felt something cool and slippery tickle her ankles as it passed by on what seemed to be a million, hairy legs. She brought herself up resting on her elbows and craning her neck to peek at her toes.

"What is your name?" she asked, smiling.

Without slowing the movement of its legs, the creature paused and looked at her curiously. "I've been named serpent. I don't know why but I intend to glorify, and with those words I'll say goodbye."

Its forked tongue advanced and retreated from its mouth and then serpent continued on.

Taking note of the position of the sun, she decided to go back to the place where she began so she could report all to God that she had done and seen. She started back toward the place where she had last seen God's face. She started toward home.

When she was nearly there, crossing her wrists like an *X*, she reached ahead and parted the tall grasses to expose the small clearing of her beginning. God sat with His back to her moving His arms back and forth in a sweeping fashion.

On her tiptoes, she thought to sneak up to Him and peek over His shoulder.

Hearing her approach, God smiled and continued with what He was doing. When she was a mere toes length away, He turned around and whisked her from her feet. She laughed as they played together. She loved God with all her heart. She looked at Him and

she saw that God was perfectly good and her spirit rose within her and acknowledged this. Yes, God was a good God.

He smiled and nodded in agreement, as though He had heard her inward declaration and then returned to His work. Once finished, He called to his daughter and stepped aside to reveal His creation.

It was a chair. A beautiful chair! With sweeping arches of color, iridescence and shimmering. "Sit here while we talk." He motioned to the chair, smiling.

How easy it was to follow the wishes of the One who loved her more than all else. She walked over slowly, admiring her Father's handiwork once again. She sat as He had instructed. She was still amazed that He had crafted this opulence for her. She rubbed the arm rest, enjoying the moment of complete satisfaction with Him.

He lowered Himself in front of her a short distance away. Then He reached for her hand, and she held it out to meet His.

"Daughter, I have much to tell you and many gifts to give you ... but today, not only will you receive these and other gifts, you will be a gift."

With that, He began to tell her more stories ...

The Father told her so many great things about this man that she stood several times as though to walk to find "him" but God tugged her back down and finished each thought carefully despite her excitement.

"The place you went today ..." He paused and made sure she was still watching Him. "Tell me, what did you think?"

Her words started slowly but sped up as her mind recounted all the bugs and snakes and tree animals she had discovered.

"Remember this well because I want you to share this with your man. After all," He said, "you will have many new things to show him." He smiled deeply at her and gave her a wink.

He went on to give her some insight about the man whom He occasionally referred to as Adam just as he occasionally referred to her as Adam. God said Adam would love her. He had told her that both she and Adam had been made in His image and He intended that they have dominion. He said Adam would have much to show her and tell her too.

About the time the sun was retreating to the far side of the earth, God told her about the secret that her body held. She was intrigued. He hadn't said much else because He "didn't want to spoil the surprise," but He told her where to direct Adam and that she and Adam could be joined.

God knew His daughter was curious, so He made sure to leave space for her to explore and discover on her own. He had created her, like man, to be inquisitive. God knew they would spend generations searching and finding, discovering and creating. That day, in the beginning, they would discover each other, but in some millennia, they would discover atoms and solar systems and … well, all that would come.

Yes, she was a suitable fit for Adam. She was a bit smaller in stature, but she held a power of mind and spirit that the man would enjoy getting to know. They could forever challenge each other as iron sharpens iron. With Adam's gifting of focus and determination and her gifting of connecting and determination, they would dominate the planet with wisdom.

God looked at her. She had discovered at least three distinct types of butterflies and was categorizing them. Yes, when He looked at her, He saw deeply, and God said it was good.

And now, near the close of the sixth day, it was time for them to meet.

Chapter 3

Oneness

Oneness. What is it?

The notion of many becoming one is common in many cultures and religions. It is the idea of university. "Uni" means one and "diversity" means many. Ergo: one out of many.

But what is oneness in the context of Christianity? How is it created? Although not wholly dissimilar in meaning for Christian and non-Christian thinkers, there is a striking difference. Notably, all Christian precepts rest in the environment God created. This foundation of God's truth is not necessarily a strong consideration when discussion of this concept occurs outside Christian circles.

To put it simply, oneness for a man is fostered by taking care of others or being the provider. A man typically considers himself one with those in a space he has created or conquered. This is different from what oneness means for a woman. She becomes one with the one who has created a space for her, and her oneness involves sex in a very potent way.

> What God has joined together in this way,
> no one may sever (Mk 10:9, The VOICE).

Whenever God speaks about becoming one flesh, the image could be of the physical uniting of two bodies. But, taken in context, we know this unity exceeds the physical. Jesus said, "What God has joined together in this way no man may sever." Do you imagine Jesus meant, once we unite sexually, we live as conjoined people? The answer is no and yes.

Think of this:

> but from the tree of the knowledge of good
> and evil you shall not eat, for in the day that you
> eat from it you will surely die (Gen 2:17, NASB)

Because we enjoy the benefit of hindsight, when we review God's warning to both Adams, clear that part of this truth rested in the natural realm - eating. What was unknown at the time was that part of this truth also rested in the spiritual realm – "You will die."

Likewise, we see the same split of natural and spiritual consequences in Genesis 2:24.

> 24 For this reason a man shall leave his
> father and his mother, and be joined to his wife;
> and they shall become one flesh. (NASB)

Part of this truth rests in the natural realm: a man leaves his father and mother and is united with his wife. But here, we see that part of this truth resides in the spiritual realm: "And the two become one flesh."

Both Scriptures refer to the physical and the spiritual.

Consider this: once an action is taken in the natural realm, a corresponding action in the spiritual realm complies. This spiritual joining is not controlled by your will. It is simply a force that women live with, the consequences of which impact her life. But this law acts regardless of her intention. It reacts only to the behavior. She has no ability to mitigate or renounce it. In the same way gravity insists a person will fall down rather than fall up, this force activates with or without her consent.

God's intention is clear. Sex was created before the fall. It was neither dull nor undesirable. It was perfect. Sex is an extraordinary gift from God to humanity. It must be respected and treasured as the powerful force that it is or, like any other unharnessed power, it can cause massive destruction.

Knowing what you know now, if you loved your life and acknowledged who you are and the fullness of your potential, it should be clear why God includes sex inside marriage but warns us to avoid it outside of marriage. God wants women to explore their gifts without the complication of an uncommitted man. God wants women to mature and cultivate a full identity of their capabilities before creating oneness with a man. God wants women to be the fullness of what they were created to be.

God has shown us His love by giving us good pleasures. Sex is pleasurable. Sex is good. Sex is fun. For women, sex creates oneness, but because of this, sex can misalign women who use it in the wrong arenas.

Imagine ...

Woman

Adam heard the song of the birds while his brain crawled up from under a deep sleep.

He raised himself up to a half reclining position. He remained in that position for a bit while debating if he should open his eyes or if he should just lie back down and try to trap the sleep that had seemingly escaped from his grasp.

Then he heard the sounds of God approaching.

God had been bringing the beasts of the field and the birds of the air to him in a seemingly endless stream. With every new creation that God showed him, Adam's excitement grew. He would give the creature a name and God would make it so. Adam enjoyed everything about the game.

His existence was everything he could wish for. Life, for that is what he called his existence, was good.

With this thought, his mind buzzed awake with activity. He jumped up in anticipation of the next creature God would bring to him.

With the sudden movement, he felt a dull pain in his side. Adam was surprised to see a movement under his skin and then, just as suddenly, the pain disappeared as if it had never existed.

He returned his attention to the area where he had heard his Father's voice.

As God approached, Adam heard God speaking and occasionally laughing.

That's strange, he thought. *Who could God be talking with?*

Adam squinted to peer deeper into the tall brush and trees from which he heard God coming. It was then that he finally saw the radiance of the Father approaching.

The biggest grin that Adam's face could muster was plastered there in response to the sight. But, again, the Father kept looking behind Himself and laughing and talking.

Finally looking up in Adam's direction, God said, "Oh, Adam, I see you are awake. I have someone I would like you to meet."

Adam was snagged on the words. "Some … one?" What could the Father mean? "Someone?" he said aloud.

Adam lowered his head and stared at the ground to mull over this new concept God had so casually tossed his way. He didn't understand it but that was the magnificence of life with the Father. Adam's entire life was filled with discovery of himself and his surroundings.

His concentration on these questions was broken by the glint of sunlight that shown through the trees in the place the Father had parted to approach where Adam was standing.

Adam looked toward God and realized the Father was hiding something behind his back.

Adam's senses were on high alert. He had known for his entire existence that God is the Father of Lights and *always* brings good gifts.

He raced toward God in a determined way, chewing up the distance between them with each long, powerful stride. Adam raced to be closer to God and to see what new creature God had brought to him to name.

Over the last few yards, Adam dropped to the ground and slid to within inches of the Father's feet, leaving a small furrow in the soil and grass shavings along the length of his body.

God let out a deep, belly laugh as He reached toward Adam to help him rise, but Adam was on his feet in the blink of an eye.

Adam joined the Father in laughing and leaned in for a long, meaningful hug. Always curious and now playful, Adam took the opportunity to peek around God for a glimpse at this creature whom God had called someone.

Just as his field of vision was about to crest the space behind God, God released Adam and stepped back, looking directly into Adam's eyes.

"In this creation before you, I have commanded the birds and creatures to be fruitful and multiply and fill the earth. This command I also give to you."

Adam bowed before God to acknowledge this command.

Upon rising, Adam stood and stared at God. Adam brought his hand to his chin and stroked his beard while he pondered how this

could be. God cocked his head slightly to the side and, with a subtle smile, watched Adam think over His latest instruction.

That is when Adam noticed movement behind the Father.

To his amazement, the most breathtaking of beings, of which he beheld now and forever, made her appearance.

His eyes were the first to be captivated by her beauty. His breathing stopped as though the air from his lungs might disturb the image on which he was transfixed.

Without thinking, he took a few steps toward her just wanting to be near her, to touch her, to know her.

She, in the same way, was captivated by Adam. God had told her that she would be pleased to meet Adam, but from His stories, she had not imagined this. To say she was pleased to meet Adam was like equating a spring shower with Victoria Falls.

In her periphery, she noticed the Father smiling and moving from between them to allow them unfettered access to one another. She smiled. Her Father was a giver of *good* gifts.

She reached out to the man who had started to approach her.

Chapter 4

Day Six

Dominion

ominion is not a word we use regularly today. In fact, some would say the thought of dominion is something to be avoided because it conveys the idea of oppressing people societies, or countries that have been colonized or exploited. This type of dominion requires the subjugation of people - not just animals or objects. Even worse, in some cases, those in the position of dominating people attempted to strip the distinction of humanity from those people surviving under their dominion. That was the experience of fallen man experting dominion. What was the experience intended to be the Adams; for those living inside the will of God? What do you think of the way God uses the word?

Let's begin with a definition.

The Hebrew word used is radah (רדה).

Strong's defines *radah* as rule *(v)*: To exert control, direction, or influence over, especially by curbing or restraining; to spread out through a land through authority or by walking among the subjects.

Another definition can be found with Brown-Driver-Briggs's Hebrew and English lexicon:

1. to rule, have dominion, dominate, tread down

1a) (*Qal*) to have dominion, rule, subjugate

1b) (*Hiphil*) to cause to dominate

2. to scrape out

2a) (*Qal*) to scrape, scrape out

In reading the definitions from both sources, I see no significant discord. It seems that God basically told the Adams to call the world into order under their vision. He wanted both of them to have authority over creation.

Read the following Scripture and think about how these verses shape the way you view God's intention of dominion.

> 26 Then God said, "Let Us make man in Our image, according to Our likeness; and let them rule over the fish of the sea and over the birds of the sky and over the cattle and over all the earth, and over every creeping thing that creeps on the earth." 27 God created man in His own image, in the image of God He created him; male and female He created them. 28 God blessed them; and God said to them, "Be fruitful and multiply, and fill the earth, and subdue it; and rule over the fish of the sea and over the birds of the sky and over every living thing that moves on the earth." (Gen 1:26–28, NASB)

But notice something that may not have caught your attention until now: "them." God gave *them* dominion over fish, the creeping things, basically everything on earth.

God did not give them dominion over each other. God did not give the male Adam dominion over the female Adam. Neither did God give the female Adam dominion over the male Adam. Both male and female were given dominion over the planet in God's establishment of a perfect hierarchy.

Now, consider this: since it is true that they held dominion together, the release of dominion to Satan requires the consent of both.

If you own property with your spouse, both owners must sign the property release in order for the property to legally transfer to the buyer. In the same way, Satan became the prince of this world when Adam *and* Woman consented to release their dominion by their disobedience.

Let this sink in. Male and female, as equal partners, were to subdue and rule this world. Male and female, as equal partners, gave the world away.

Having learned more about God's intended implementation of dominion, let's rejoin Man and Woman on their last days of full obedience to the Living God.

Imagine ...

Naked and Unashamed

Opening her eyes, she was greeted with the decadent beauty that was her world. This is where she was going to be forever, and the richness of it all enveloped her like a velvety cocoon.

She smiled as she felt Adam's hand shifting slightly on her hip while he slept, folded onto her body.

It had been a glorious day although the sun had yet to rise.

She smiled as she recounted the events of the sixth day—the day of their creation.

As if in a trance, Adam had walked toward her. His mouth was slightly ajar and his eyes scanned her face and body, taking in every inch of her being.

He continued to come closer, mesmerized, an engine of curiosity powering his movements. As he reached her, Adam ignored her outstretched arms. He hadn't seen them.

She stood there staring at him, equally enthralled, but her feet seemed fixed in this spot in the garden. She smiled as he approached. She was eager to talk with him but he seemed focused on her body, her exterior. His reaction was a little unexpected since the Father had told her the man would love her. Looking at his face, she wasn't sure she saw love, but she did see that he wanted to know her and that was enough. For now.

She wanted to know him too. She wondered what his voice sounded like and what he was thinking.

He stopped when he stood between her outstretched arms. His stare was intense but she had no fear.

She let her arms fall, dangling at her side, tilted her head and smiled. "I'm very pleased to meet you," she said.

Still, he stood there saying nothing but clearly, thoughts were racing through his mind. She couldn't know his thoughts but she did perceive that he was thinking.

Before God brought her to Adam for introduction, He had told her to be patient with this man. Even though only a few breaths had passed, it was difficult to stand in one place and be patient but she remained - just as God had reminded her.

At last, inches from her face, Adam opened his mouth to speak. His spirit was overwhelmed by her presence and no sound escaped even though he thought he had willed his voice to be. Instead, as was the case when he needed God, the Father filled his open mouth.

"This one, at last, is bone of my bone and flesh of my flesh. This one will be called Woman or Isha, for she was taken from man (from Ish). This is why a man leaves his father and mother and bonds with his wife, and they become one flesh." With these words, they were betrothed.

As she felt his warm breath battle with the heat of the day on her skin, she thought this man was so different from her … but she was already thinking how fun it would be to get to know him.

She made a mental note to ask what a mother and father were.

She thought to take a step backward to allow the breeze to move between them. She let her hands grab his, as she created the distance. Holy Spirit passed between them as a gentle wind. Adam finally seemed to come back to himself. He shed his mechanical movements and squeezed her hands. He smiled and then laughed out loud.

"Isha, you are more beautiful than the sky as the sun rises or sets." Having been called Isha, she knew that that meant Adam was Ish.

"Thank you," she said. Woman felt a growing awareness in her soul that she would be with Adam forever.

She shook her head and laughed loudly. "Ish, come with me. I want to share something with you."

She already held his hands in hers. She dropped them, turned. and ran toward the outer spot in the garden.

Her speed surprised even her, as she sprinted through the tall trees. She ran quickly to bring Adam to her discovery as much as to shake off the strange and wonderful sensations that seemed to vibrate her entire self from the inside out.

She heard his footfalls behind her. He could have easily caught up to her and passed her, but he ran behind her. That thought alone was enough to propel her even faster toward their destination.

"Isha," he panted, "where are you taking us?"

"Not many more steps," she yelled over her shoulder. Woman was determined to keep some distance between them so she could watch the wonder in his face when she revealed the place to which God had guided her on the sixth day.

She slowed down as she got closer. She didn't hear him running behind her any longer.

She looked back while as she walked, craning her neck to see if she could catch a glimpse of his head above the grasses and undergrowth.

She was nearly there. She'd wanted him to be here now, but he must have paused to catch his breath.

She waited … and waited, scanning the trees and grasses … and waited.

Finally, she heard him. She saw the flowers first and then his head. "Iiiiishshaaaaa," he sang, "beautiful cree-chah."

Adam had put an unimaginable number of flowers into his thick hair so the flowers protruded like a mane of blossoms. Yes, Woman thought, he was very different. Adam strode toward her. His smile was intoxicating. He continued singing, not well, but his joy was contagious.

He grabbed her hand and pulled her toward him, still singing. "So glad to meee-chah!" he sang louder and louder, while they spun on the carpet of deep green grass.

He slowly stopped spinning and, once again, with a distant yet focused look in his eye, came close to her. Pulling the flowers from his hair, one at a time, he gave them to her.

He didn't know why he thought she would like them but the delicate beauty of the flowers very much reminded him of her delicate beauty. He wanted to share them and all of himself with her.

She smiled, thanking him for the armful of flowers.

He watched as the flowers tumbled from the safety of her arms to the ground as she turned. She grabbed his hands once again, and pulled him toward the edge of the tall grasses.

She parted the grasses for him and he finally saw what she wanted to share with him. He was overwhelmed by the extravagance of the place. So much life! And … how did she know of it? He turned to her astonished that she knew something he did not yet know. He

turned toward her and was immediately inundated with the happiness of being with her.

Crossing the last of the tall grasses, Woman pulled him to the ground, not far from the edge of the clearing. Sitting, she had pushed her hair away from her face.

He'd noticed everything about her. The hair on her head was dark and curly, the hair under her arms was straight and the hair in other places was somewhere in between. He would have to give God extra praise when they walked together at the end of the day, the next morning.

He leaned to the side and rested his weight on his elbow causing him to sink slightly into the fertile soil. They started talking. Both were amazed to see so many creatures in one place.

As the creatures emerged, Adam told Isha what he had named each of them. She memorized the names quickly and recalled the names in their later discussions. Adam found this amazing!

Adam told story after story. They were fully involved in enjoying each other. Finally, he told Woman how he had named so many creatures his creativity had been stretched. They laughed until their sides were sore when Adam tried to describe one of the creatures he had struggled to name. He described a creature that resembled a body with ad hoc parts, long nose, short ears and stumpy body.

"After a while, I just looked at God and said, 'Aardvark." Adam said. "Spare body parts; spare vowels." Adam roared at his own joke, rolling backward in utter abandonment to his humor.

The sun's position in the sky gave way to the advancing moon and still they talked. Their conversations dove deeply into their passionate love for the Father and talking without end about what it was like to first behold God's face. They talked about what it was like to have dominion but then they decided to discuss the topic further when the sun next returned. Then the conversation turned to what each of them expected in anticipation of meeting the other and how they felt when God introduced them.

Woman and Adam had spent hours gazing at, touching and discovering each other. They talked and laughed and touched. As the day continued, she had decided to reveal the secret to Adam.

Remembering God's cloaked instruction, she helped Adam discover the secret she held within her body.

From that moment until now, they were one—inseparable. Ish and Isha. Husband and wife.

*****

Now, on day seven, she let out a quiet chuckle just remembering how they both were so surprised at what their bodies could do.

But, enough of that. Right now, she wanted to explore more around her.

God had proclaimed day seven a day of rest. She and Adam would surely find many things to do while resting on that day.

God told her that Adam had been assigned the task of cultivating the garden. Her task was to be an *ezer* to Adam. God had instilled in her a confidence, such that she was sure she would be able to complete her task.

"But what is an *ezer*?" she wondered. God said it was a strong, insightful ally but God had also said a suitable fit and protector.

She was learning that her Father was full of mystery, always willing to share and always giving good gifts.

She looked over at Adam, who was sleeping, and drank in his entire being with her eyes and then her touch. At some point during her exploration, Adam woke up. Pulling her to him, they journeyed to that place of physical oneness, discovering each other and generating an enthusiastic, embrace of obedience and a raucous expression of thankfulness to the Father for His good gifts.

The Day Before

Adam sought the Father's heart as he made a plan to cultivate and maintain that piece of paradise. "Your will" were the only words God spoke to him as they walked together. Peace enveloped Adam's soul, as the Father thumped him soundly on the shoulder and followed up with a squeeze.

"The earth is yours. The two of you have been given dominion. Create. Saturate. Dominate. This is your destiny." God's words not only resounding in Adam's ears but from deep within himself and rippling outward.

Feeling a surge of confidence, Adam turned to behold God's face. God stopped and fully faced the man. His spirit overwhelmed by the greatness, vastness and fullness of the being in whose image he had been made. Adam was made radiant. Transformed once again, he experienced the indescribable oneness between the Creator and created.

"My will, my will," Adam repeated.

Earlier in the morning, he had thought to ask this personal question of the Father while he was alone with him but now he wanted Isha to be there too.

Adam, completely refreshed and with renewed purpose, continued to develop the plan that had begun with his will. As he jogged to where he had left Isha to enjoy the breaking of the overnight fast, he grinned with anticipation. He would get great pleasure from sharing God's words with her on the way to their spot of working that day.

After working from morning to nearly evening, they were weary in body but their spirits refused to recognize that call. Having chosen to cultivate the outer place she had shown him on day six, they worked to make sure the serene area of the clearing remained just that—clear. They spent time gathering fruit from the nearby trees and enjoyed lunch and conversation and yet another act (or two) in their unrelenting quest to be fruitful (and of course obedient).

Shortly after the midday meal, Isha felt a need to relieve herself. She hesitated trying to think of a way not to make a mess. Again, she was unsuccessful. Isha decided she needed a plan to manage the

liquid and solids that were regularly expelled from their bodies. She mentioned this to Adam.

Adam had gladly shown her how he projected the liquid from his outer tube. He tended to project the stream at random targets and had even jokingly challenged Isha to a duel, but she had no outer tubing.

After some hunting and discovery, Ish and Isha decided they would take it upon themselves to reveal the mystery of her tubing, which was invisible at a cursory look.

Isha had taken to expelling liquids in the stream since she did not like the warm fluid running down her legs and across her feet and toes. To no avail, she had tried to give the stream some direction away from her legs but unable to see that part of her body, she could only feel her way around. The mess left by that experiment was even more distasteful than doing nothing.

After a day of working, they returned to the spot they called home. It was near a stream to allow her to expel her body water in comfort.

Since it was evening, they decided to begin the day by finally uncovering the mystery of Isha's water tube. After a meal of fruit and nuts, she asked Ish to look for her water tube. He was in perpetual discovery mode, and because of the proximity of the water tube to the pleasure area that could make them fruitful, *as God commanded,* he didn't even bother to ask questions before hustling toward her as she lay back and relaxed her legs.

After looking more closely, he sat back in surprise. He had such a large water tube and hers was, well, paltry. Of course, Adam hadn't let his opportunity pass to engage his water tube for its other purpose. Even so, they said this was another discussion to be had with God but, in light of the experience of the latter, it just didn't seem that important at the moment.

They settled in for the night and rested until morning.

*****

Over the next few days, they settled into a pattern of coming in from the day's work area. More times than not, they gravitated toward the middle of the garden, beginning their days at the place where the Tree of Life and the Tree of the Knowledge of Good and Evil were both easily in view.

The day before, they had devised a game where one would hide while the other sought them out. Once found, the finder would take the fruit of the tree or bush and toss it to the other, as if tossing a baseball. This was one of the fun methods they used to gather dinner to start the day. They were usually quite hungry from working all day.

Woman was the first to hide. She was lithe enough to become invisible once sidled next to a butter fruit tree. But, even in the noisiness of Eden, Adam found her quickly. He tossed her the butter fruit and ran off to hide. This went on for a few rounds.

Eventually, Isha found herself searching for Ish again. She called out to him for quite a while, and hearing her stomach growl loudly, she concluded that this game should end early. She laughed and called to Ish once more, announcing she was going to eat all they had gathered unless he made himself appear.

Adam laughed so loudly she knew immediately where he stood. Right behind her!

With a grin, she spun around to face him. The smile melted from her face. Horrified, she saw him leaning against the tree in the middle of the garden.

"Noooo" she yelled, charging toward him, hoping against hope that she could get his hand from the tree before he fell over dead.

The smile fell from Adam's face as he saw Isha rushing him with her head bowed as though she would ram right through him. He removed his hand from the trunk of the tree. "What?"

That was the single word that escaped his body before the full force of her charge punched into his belly. He was catapulted several feet beyond where he had once stood.

Though dazed by the impact, she was up and running to him within seconds. She checked his hands, looked into his eyes, and watched him … live. Confused, she looked at him.

"You're …" She staggered backward a few steps. "You're not dead!" she yelled with the beginning of a smile as incredulity rushed through her mind.

He didn't understand her confusion. Lying on the ground, he simply stared back at her until he had the presence of mind to say, "What was *that* all about?"

"God said we shall surely die … if we touch the tree or eat of its fruit," she said breathlessly, her adrenaline rush beginning to wane.

"No, Isha." Adam corrected. "God said we will surely die if we *eat* of its fruit."

She shook her head violently. "No, Ish. *Eat or touch.*"

"He told me that I should not eat of the Tree of the Knowledge of Good and Evil or I will surely die." Adam insisted.

"Did you say the Tree of the Knowledge of Good and Evil?" she asked. Her curiosity rushed toward the new information.

"Yes," Adam said as he stood up and walked back to the fruit they had gathered for dinner.

Woman pondered this for a moment. *The tree in the middle of the garden is the Tree of the Knowledge of Good and Evil?* She closed her eyes tightly and squished her mouth and nose together in puzzlement.

And Adam can touch this tree but I cannot? These new thoughts chased one another in an endless cycle like a dog hopelessly trying to catch its tail.

After a few more cycles, the violence of these thoughts had begun to drill into the fabric of her trust in God's faithfulness – but just a little. This miniscule thinning in the God-strengthened veil that shielded her from the evil forces that moved in and out of the garden was quickly recognized by the enemy. This was the opportunity to plant the seed that he had planted in the hearts of so many angels in a time before.

A hot wind upset the dust directly to her left. She glanced over her shoulder but saw nothing save the usually talkative but harmless serpent. The enemy's seed settled into the thinning and created a space for itself in her heart.

Her stomach growled loudly once more and, obedient to its call, Woman hurried over to where Adam had arranged the meal. They greeted each other again, blessed the meal and ate until they were filled.

As was their custom, they preferred to sleep wrapped in each other's arms. Ish and Isha had no idea that the enemy had plans for the seed now planted in the woman's inner workings.

The enemy would execute his plan once they woke in the morning. He just needed to put the plan in motion before God came to be with them in the cool of the day.

Chapter 5

Deceived

Why did Satan choose Woman to deceive? Have you ever asked yourself this question? If Satan needed to choose between Man and Woman, why Woman?

> And it was not Adam who was deceived, but the woman who was deceived and fell into transgression. (1 Tim 2:14, BSB)

Growing up in church, I heard many preachers attempt to answer the question of why Woman was deceived rather than Adam. Some posit that Satan chose her because she was less knowledgeable. Having been created after Adam, she was more naïve and, therefore, easier to deceive.

I heard other sermons that argued that Woman was simply not as well equipped intellectually. These sermons were built on the false assumption that God never spoke to Woman, only to Adam. These sermons presumed that any knowledge Woman had came from Adam, not God.

More recently, I have heard sermons that argue that Adam retained responsibility for the fall because he was the leader of the couple. This argument says that the fall of humanity occurred when the leader disobeyed God. It presumes that the Woman's disobedience did not affect the condition of the world because she had a lesser role.

I am certain you have also heard a gambit of reasons Woman was deceived. I have only listed a few.

It is not my intention to refute each argument. I choose to address the assumption of Woman's ignorance. This idea has insidious repercussions on the way we form our ideas of what it means to be a girl or woman. With this in mind, let's begin our review of this idea.

The most popular assumption is that Woman wasn't as smart as Adam. It has been ingrained into many cultures over the centuries before and after Christ.

It is important to remember that men held positions of power for many centuries. This fact does not implicate men as culprits or villains; however, it does mean that many of our Christian ideals and traditions are filtered through the male perspective.

You may have heard of the Christian principle of Sola Scriptura. This means that only Holy Scripture contains the truths needed for our salvation and spiritual life. It is the only infallible Word of God. This belief admits that tradition and church and denominational doctrines cannot be considered sound if there is a contradiction with the Bible. This is also the basis of our discussion.

When necessary, we will spend time identifying areas of Christian belief compared to the verses contained in God's Word. In the process, we will begin to expose a bias in the way God's Word has been translated and interpreted. We will break apart any thought-pairs that are invalid from a biblical perspective. By examining the interpretation of the creation story and comparing it to the written Word, truth will reveal itself.

In biblical times, the unfortunate reality is that women were considered to be less than equal to men. In many cases, this resulted in a limited formal education for women. Women were taught to focus primarily on home and family. This lack of equality also resulted in many women not being treasured as full partners in humanity.

This miseducation of women resulted in the self-perpetuating behaviors and cultural reinforcements that continue even now in some branches of the church. This thought that women are not equal partners of men is a foundational idea and many consider it to be a "traditional" Christian value.

For nearly a century, this thought has come under assault by leaders outside the church. In recent years, the doctrine of inequality has come under scrutiny from inside the Church as well. These assumptions of inequity made by Church leadership regarding Woman's dim-wittedness or naïve ignorance are truly low-hanging fruit (excuse the pun) when we consider logical reasons Woman was the target of the enemy's deception.

I think Woman was selected for precisely the opposite reason. It was her intellect and way of thinking that made her the preferred target. The enemy used her God-given gifts of insight and sensitivity to subtlety engage her vast abilities and manipulate her, and subsequently the man, to induce humanity's destruction.

The Difference

Consider the instructions God gave each of them about the tree whose fruit was never to be encountered.

Adam and Woman are warned that the tree would cause their death if they did not heed God's command.

Notice how God described the forbidden tree to each of them. He doesn't give them the same description. God described the tree to Adam by saying the tree was "the tree of knowledge of good and evil." God described the tree to Woman by saying "the tree that is in the middle of the garden."

Examine the other difference in the instructions God gave them. God told Adam that he may not eat of the tree and the consequence of eating the fruit of the tree. He told Woman that she may not eat from the tree or *touch* the tree.

> but from the tree of the knowledge of good and evil you shall not eat, for in the day that you eat from it you will surely die." (Gen 2:17, NASB)

> but from the fruit of the tree which is in the
> middle of the garden, God has said, 'You shall
> not eat from it or touch it, or you will die'. (Gen
> 3:3, NASB)

When I first saw this in Scripture, I asked some highly respected people in my life their opinions on the discrepancy. A common response was that Woman had mistakenly added "touch" to the instruction.

I suppose it could be true, except, this would be a unique way to interpret Scripture.

Let's take a moment to determine if this is one of the biases in how we understand Scripture.

God Said

In Genesis 3:3, Woman says, "God said." Then she describes God's instructions to her. Other than her recollection, we have no record of this conversation she remembers having with God.

But why do we presume she is mistaken in her recollection? What is it about her that would require us to question her truthfulness or accuracy? She says that God told her not to touch or eat from the tree, but rather than believe her, our Christian teachings discount her words. Why? What is the background narrative that drives us to believe something other than God's words from her mouth?

Up to this point, we have no scriptural basis on which to question her integrity. In rejecting Woman's truthfulness, it seems we have accepted a deviation from the Holy Scripture. This subtle error is quite substantial. It contorts God's Word to fit the unspoken hypothesis that both Adam and Woman were given the same instructions.

Rather than accepting what the Bible actually says, many of us have bound together two ideas: 1) the inferiority of her understanding and 2) that God gave the same instructions to both male and female. Uncouple these thoughts and accept that Woman was being accurate.

What is it about this bias that causes discomfort for some when we are forced to accept the truth? Is it because we have a bias to believe God must provide the same instructions to both the male and female Adam? If so, why would we make such a presumption?

If you are a parent of children with wildly differing personalities or talents, do you give them identical instructions? Usually not. There are general instructions that you give to both children; however, due to their personality, character, or innate traits, a wise parent customizes the instruction given so each child can benefit fully.

Imagine you have two children, Campbell and Taylor. Both had been playing with their toys but have moved into a different room without putting their toys away. When you enter the room, you notice toys on the floor but no children playing.

You call them back into the room and instruct them to pick up the toys. This is the common instruction given regardless of each child's talents.

In this same way, God gave Adam and Woman a common instruction. This tree will cause your death if you disobey my command.

Then there are instructions given because the parent knows the way of the child, how each child thinks.

Let's revisit the room with toys on the floor. Imagine both children are returning to the room to pick up the toys. Campbell enters before Taylor. You point to a toy car located in the pathway between you and the door, taking the opportunity to teach Campbell the reason it is important to put toys away.

"Campbell, when you left the car in the middle of the floor, I could have stepped on it and hurt my foot. Not only could I have hurt my foot, the wheels on the car could have caused me to lose my balance. I could have careened across the floor and fallen, hurting myself." While speaking to Campbell, you make a careening motion with your foot and body and pretend to fall to the floor and hurt yourself.

As you talk, you look into Campbell's face and see that this child is imagining the destruction and pain that the toy could have caused you had you stepped on it. You *know* Campbell. You *know*

Campbell will try very hard in the future to put the toys away so that no harm comes to you.

In the same way, God gave Adam a detailed description of the tree he was to avoid eating. God *knew* that Adam would not want to disobey his Father. God *knew* Adam would focus only on the fact that the tree was forbidden. God *knew* that knowing the name of the tree would not be a temptation to Adam. Adam did not process this information in the same way as Woman.

Your other child, Taylor, enters the room. While Campbell continues picking up toys and putting them away, you take the same teaching opportunity with Taylor but, due to Taylor's proclivities, you take a different approach.

"Taylor, when you left the car in the middle of the floor, someone could have stepped on it and hurt themselves. Be careful to put all of your toys back into the proper place so no one steps on your toys and breaks the toy or injures themselves."

You look into Taylor's face and see that this child has also heard your words and will try hard in the future to put the toys away so no harm comes to anyone else.

You have arrived at identical outcomes. Both children now understand why they should put their toys away; however, the teaching method was different because your children are different.

As a parent, you *know* Taylor. You *know* the teaching approach with Taylor could not include a role play of your careening across the floor aboard a child's toy car. Had you given Taylor this detailed description of the perils of leaving a toy in the middle of the floor, Taylor would have been tempted to create the scenario, not out of evil intention but out of curiosity. Taylor would have wanted to see if a toy car could cause a person to speed across the room. For this reason, you omitted that level of detail.

Possibly for the same reason, God omitted the description of the tree in His instruction to Woman. Instead, He chose to call the tree to her attention by describing its location: "the tree in the middle of the garden." This description did not trigger any further thought. It did not cause her to ponder the tree. This description simply told her the location of the tree she was to avoid eating or touching.

If you are not a parent, I'm sure you have friends who are very different. You likely have a friend you can share your heart with and be confident that your words are sealed within their soul. You may have another friend who you value equally but you *know* this friend. You are very general or discreet with information that you do not wish not to be shared with others inside or outside your circle.

Let's be bold. Let's choose not to ascribe error, lying or embellishment as a pre-fall trait to Adam or Woman. Let's discard the unsubstantiated assumption that Adam was her only vehicle to gain knowledge. Let's choose to believe that when Woman said, "God said," she did so because she had heard God speak.

It is important to notice how God tailored His speech to His audience. When speaking to Woman, God omits the descriptive name of the tree. Why did God do this? I think, as her Creator, God knew the power He had placed inside her. God knew of her ability to "see." In His wisdom, this omission let her curiosity remain inert. In this way, Woman did not focus her *ra'ah* on the one forbidden tree of the garden.

Ra'ah

The Hebrew word used in Scripture to describe Woman's ability to see is *ra'ah*.

Let's dive deeper here. God created Woman so she could "see" without making an effort.

> And the woman seeth [ra'ah] that the tree [is] good for food, and that it [is] pleasant to the eyes, and the tree is desirable to make [one] wise, (Gen 3:6a, YLT)

Until the moment Woman looks at the fruit of the forbidden tree, the word *ra'ah* is used only when God assesses His handiwork and when God waits "to see" what Adam will name the animals.

She is the first being in God's creation to see as God saw. She was the first human to *ra'ah*.

This kind of "seeing" is not merely viewing an object in your field of vision with your eyes. This is seeing an object and perceiving a deeper understanding about the character of the object with your mind or possibly with your spirit.

Here is a quick review of Hebrew. Remember Hebrew is read right to left. In Hebrew script, each letter has a meaning. Words form pictures by linking the letters.

The ancient Hebrew spelling of ra'ah is רָאָה—reysh (ר), alef (א), hey (ה).

Now that we have seen the word in modern Hebrew, let's review it in ancient Hebrew: 𐤓𐤀𐤄

Hey began as a drawing of a person with arms raised. *Alef* began as a drawing of the head of an ox. *Reysh* began as a drawing of a person's head.

Think of what these symbols could mean.

Hey (𐤄) To reveal; behold
Alef (𐤀) Strong; leader; first
Reysh (𐤓) the chief; the head; a person

As mentioned before, Hebrew can have layered meanings, so now that we know the meanings of each letter, let's resume study of this word in the way we examined *ezer* earlier.

The first and second letters + the third letter —𐤓+𐤀𐤄

𐤀𐤄 to see or perceive; to see a vision.
𐤓 the chief or person
is a person to see or behold a vision; to perceive a revelation.
The first letter + the second third letters — 𐤄𐤀 + 𐤓
𐤓 the chief or person
𐤄𐤀 strong revelation. This word is translated as a strong sigh.

We see that *ra'ah* is a primary person with a depth of insight
Think of the picture given to us.
Ra'ah, רָאָה, is the highest strength of revelation.
There is seeing … and then there is "seeing."

Let's look at how *ra'ah*, to see, is used to describe how God saw.

> And God seeth (ra'ah) the light that [it is] good, and God separateth between the light and the darkness, (Gen 1:4, YLT)
>
> And God saith, `Let the waters under the heavens be collected unto one place, and let the dry land be seen **(ra'ah):**' and it is so. (Gen 1:9, YLT)
>
> And God calleth to the dry land Earth,' and to the collection of the waters He hath called `Seas;' and God seeth **(ra'ah)** that [it is] good (Gen 1:10, YLT)
>
> And the earth bringeth forth tender grass, herb sowing seed after its kind, and tree making fruit (whose seed [is] in itself) after its kind; and God seeth (ra'ah) that [it is] good; (Gen 1:12, YLT) and to rule over day and over night, and to make a separation between the light and the darkness; and God seeth (ra'ah) that [it is] good; (Gen 1:18, YLT)
>
> And God prepareth the great monsters, and every living creature that is creeping, which the waters have teemed with, after their kind, and every fowl with wing, after its kind, and God seeth (ra'ah) that [it is] good. (Gen 1:21, YLT)
>
> And God maketh the beast of the earth after its kind, and the cattle after their kind, and every creeping thing of the ground after its kind, and God seeth (ra'ah) that [it is] good. (Gen 1:25, YLT)
>
> And God seeth (ra'ah) all that He hath done, and lo, very good; and there is an evening, and there is a morning—day the sixth. (Gen 1:31, YLT)

> And Jehovah God formeth from the ground every beast of the field, and every fowl of the heavens, and bringeth in unto the man, to see (ra'ah) what he doth call it; and whatever the man calleth a living creature, that [is] its name. (Gen 2:19, YLT)

I think what we are understanding in Woman is what some have coined *intuition*. I do not define *ra'ah* as intuition. Intuition is too small to describe this defining ability.

Can you imagine that God used His intuition when He saw (*ra'ah*) all He had done in six days and said, "It was very good"? That is laughable. God used His knowledge of the seen and unseen to declare and recognize this good state of being.

This God-given ability to *ra'ah* was the very talent that the enemy used against Woman. Satan selected Woman as his target not because she was less than but precisely because her talents differed from Adam's. Her talent enabled her to decipher subtleties that may have gone unnoticed by her counterpart.

This incredible ability to plan, forecast and strategize could also be twisted to be susceptible to the wiles of the enemy *if* she ever doubted God's perfect intentions.

Woman, in her perfect creation, saw (*ra'ah*) with an insight that God ingrained in her as He crafted her from man's side. She perceived the unseen. She grappled with thoughts that eluded the five senses.

Stop here and ingest this truth.

Let's return to 1 Timothy 2:14.

Imagine with me that you are looking at a peach for the first time. Envision the fruit hanging from a tree branch. What do you see? The peach has fuzzy skin. Is the peach orange and yellow with a tinge of tan or brown? Do you see the stem sticking up from the top of the peach?

Remember in this scenario, you have never tasted a peach before so this is totally new to you. Tell me, just by looking at it, what does it taste like? Is it sweet? Tart? What is the flesh like? Is it firm like coconut? Mushy like kiwi? Does it have pulp like an orange? Does it have vitamin C, D, E? Inside the fruit, is it segmented like a grape-fruit? Does it have a core like an apple? Is it juicy like a strawberry? By looking at the peach from the outside without tasting it and without touching it, *ra'ah* the peach.

> And it was not Adam who was deceived, but the woman who was deceived and fell into trans-gression. (1 Tim 2:14, BSB)
> And the woman seeth [ra'ah] that the tree [is] good for food, and that it [is] pleasant to the eyes, and the tree is desirable to make [one] wise, (Gen 3:6a, YLT)

It is true that Woman was deceived. It is also true that she was deceived because she saw that the fruit would increase the knowledge she already possessed. Scripture says she saw that the fruit was good to make a person wise.

When she *ra'ah* the fruit, she saw much more than you or I can see when we look at our imaginary peach. Understand this, when she looked at the fruit, it was a supernatural experience. More than eyes glimpsing or studying an object. Woman saw *into* the fruit and recognized its potential.

Imagine that—Woman looked at an object and saw potential. Do you know of any women who can see potential when others see nothing?

Now, at the close of this discussion of Woman's talents, it's time to experience that fateful day when paradise was lost …

Imagine …

The Fall

Angel of Light

He was cast out of heaven and, full of rage at his defeat, trained his sights on the garden God had created. Finally, he had found a chance to strike a blow to God through the very beings God had created. As much as he dared, Satan had exploited the one chance for which he had been waiting.

In an earlier time, he had bowed his knee to the One whom the man and woman now called Father.

"Father," he mouthed the word, unable to say it aloud. The word would never cross his lips, and it was bitter in his mouth.

He had served the Eternal One but even in his days of dedicated service, he was never entitled to call God Father! His hatred for the couple in the garden ticked up a notch, although he couldn't have imagined that was possible.

Lucifer had been beautiful, until sin was found in him. He was the most beautiful, with music in his body but, his face twisted oddly at the thought that God had chosen to give dominion to them, dominion had been given to humanity. It belonged to those created in the image of the Eternal One. That seed of distaste festered until it germinated into full-blown rebellion. Lucifer, the Angel of Light, decided he would no longer serve the Most High. The Eternal had showed favor to them. "THEM!" So, Satan would use his time to rip as many of them as he could from …

"Father," he said bitterly. There, he had allowed the word to cross his lips and regretted it immediately. Now the bitterness that had been trapped in his mouth dripped down his chin.

He turned his head to spit.

Then he wiped the froth from his mouth with his forearm and the back of his hand. Gazing up at the darkened heavens, he planted his feet and bounded into the air, lifted by the evil wind beneath his wings.

After having used his influence to plant the same distrust and resentment toward the Father in a number of his fellow angelic creations, those beings had also fallen and became demons. They joined

him now. All were propelled by the desire for revenge on the Father and the destruction of his chosen.

With a sole focus, Satan set his face against the stinging barrier between the spiritual and the natural realm. He was near them. He could feel the presence and power of those made in God's image. There, in the distance, Eden came into view.

Deceived

On a day like any other, Adam woke Isha with a handful of nuts and crushed herbs.

It was still early in the morning and the sun had yet to rise.

Isha, feeling as though something was amiss, stood up and smiled at her love. This life was better than anything she could have imagined for herself. She and Adam had talked about God's commandment to be fruitful and they were fully committed to follow it. She smiled again.

Ignoring breakfast, she turned to take in the beauty of their domain.

Having just arrived from his rushed travel through the darkness, the evil one raced to fill the serpent's body and exploit what he saw as his chance to destroy God's chosen.

"Woman," the evil one called through the serpent, "Shalom."

"Shalom," Woman responded without turning to face the creature, already thinking of the day ahead. She reached down for some nuts.

"Ah, breakfast," the serpent continued. "Have you considered this tree? It is good for food."

Finally, glancing toward the serpent, she noticed he was speaking of the tree in the middle of the garden. "No, not that tree," she said. She turned her back to the evil one once again as she tossed a few nuts into her mouth and crunched noisily.

The evil one countered in a voice as innocent as he could muster, "Indeed. Did God really say you will not eat from all the trees of the garden?"

The woman stopped chewing and swallowed. She stood, walked over to the serpent, and spoke directly to it. "From the fruit of the trees of the garden we may eat," she said, "but from the fruit of the tree which is in the middle of the garden, God has said, 'You shall not eat from it or touch it, or …'"

"you will die" they said as the serpent chimed in finishing her sentence with her.

She stared at the serpent. It did not seem as innocent as in times before. Something was amiss.

Not wanting to be too obvious, the evil one pushed the character of the serpent forward and it spoke in the common inanity and cleverness to which Woman was accustomed. Woman relaxed and seemed to be satisfied.

Seizing the opportunity, the serpent said, "You will not surely die! "For God knows that in the day you eat from this tree your eyes will be opened, and you will be like God, knowing good and evil."

Peering at the serpent, Woman didn't see past its silly antics of dancing in front of her because she was distracted by the evil one's words that rang in her ears as if true as she remembered the evening Adam had leaned against the tree.

Could the serpent be correct? Again, remembering Adam had touched the tree and yet still lived.

She looked over as Adam approached her but her mind was not on him. Her thoughts were under attack. She turned back to the serpent.

Her spirit sprang into action and countered the argument by pointing out that Adam had been commanded not to *eat* of the fruit. She, on the other hand, had been admonished not to touch the tree or eat its fruit.

Standing just out of the reach of the tree and the fruit, Woman was immobile.

Her eyes were transfixed on the fruit nestled between its leaves. Her mind ran a thousand scenarios of which only a few could have been good. But the evil one, having studied God's chosen, had already harvested a fruit from the tree and now prompted her again, balancing the beautiful tiny fruit atop its head and making its way toward to her.

Still, she did not run. She did not back away. Instead, for the first time since creation, she fastened her attention to the forbidden fruit and *ra'ah*, she perceived, saw deeply and understood. In this tiny fruit, she saw the immaterial ability to think and calculate. She saw the strength to judge and to *know*.

Recognizing that Woman now understood the truth that the fruit of the tree held a path to untapped knowledge, the serpent slowly and deliberately moved forward once again, this time, remaining silent.

In fact, all of darkness held its breath. This was the moment, since the fall of Lucifer and the other darkened angels, that would allow them a chance to take dominion over the divine creation. This was their chance to derail the Eternal One's grand plan.

Isha's mind raced to process all of the information she now had. She tried to pull her eyes from the fruit but her gaze seemed set. She noticed everything about the fruit. She could *ra'ah* the knowledge plumping up the flesh of the fruit waiting impatiently for her to break the skin and drink of its juices. She understood how this deeper ability to think would allow her to perceive things that were outside the realm she lived in at that moment.

If she took part of this fruit, could she be a better *ezer* to Ish? With the knowledge of good and evil, she could protect him and be an even stronger ally. The spirit of the evil one tossed the thoughts to her silently through the door of doubt, which she was opening wider.

Never having left them alone, the Holy Spirit rushed in and raised up a standard to hold back the forces of evil arriving like a flood and gathering in an innumerable mass writhing in their closest attempt at joy at the thought of destroying the pinnacle God's creation.

With a wave of a hand, Holy Spirit silenced those demons Woman had not already allowed into her presence. But, Holy Spirit could do nothing to the evil one who now had a foothold in her heart.

As a wind coming between the serpent, the fruit and Woman, Holy Spirit reminded Woman, "The Father has given you all good gifts."

"Yes," she said. Her mind broke ranks with her eyes and wandered back toward her place with Father.

Hearing Woman utter this word, the serpent shuddered with anticipation. The movement recaptured Woman's attention, and she reached for the fruit.

Deciding. She, unknowingly but sufficiently, limited Holy Spirit's ability to shield her from destruction. Her hand moved across the few inches of distance to reach the fruit the serpent had balanced atop its head. She snatched up the fruit quickly as if to outrun the death she was bringing on herself.

In the instant the Woman's body touched the fruit, the spirit that worked to renew the garden debris froze in place. This spirit, Badaq, was confused. Badaq's work was being corrupted. Having always been present in the garden as a servant in the cycle of life, Badaq had worked in tangent with the chosen as they cultivated Eden.

As the couple chopped down trees and replanted grasses and moved budding flowers, Badaq had been faithful to begin the process of recycling the debris so it could be used for the life that remained and abounded.

Fruit and herbs died as God's chosen consumed them, but Badaq never touched the chosen ones. They lived outside his domain, separated from Badaq because they were spiritually eternal with God.

But now, with Woman's disobedience, Badaq felt a new power rising. It gnarled Badaq appearance and added to the perversion of purpose. Badaq, fully depraved, became Death and Death, now unrestrained for her, set his sights on Woman.

With the woman's will rising strongly against God's command, the trio evil spirits—Disappointment, Despair, and Discouragement—struggled past the gale that Holy Spirit held against the gathering evil. They, too, crept toward Woman.

Holding the tiny fruit in her hand, she remembered the Father's words: "But from the fruit of the tree which is in the midst of the garden, you will not eat of it, and you will not touch, otherwise you will die."

But she had done it. She had touched the fruit just as she had seen Adam do so many times ... and yet there she stood ... alive. Without thinking any further, she brought the fruit to her mouth. Hesitating only for a breath, she opened her mouth, pressed the skin of the succulent fruit to her teeth and took a bite.

Surprised by the lack of brilliant flavor she had expected, she felt immediate disappointment. She chewed absentmindedly on the flesh as she brought the fruit before her eyes to inspect its exposed flesh.

A few drops of juice dotted the fruit's skin at the place she had bitten. Looking at it, she *ra'ah* that the fruit was good to make them wise, but she had expected she would feel something else. She felt nothing new. Death, corrupted and depraved and with a new freedom to affect God's chosen, now stood before the woman to devour her. Death watched and waited impatiently as her spirit slowly began to die, separating from God's Spirit.

"Isha," a voice whispered breathlessly at her shoulder. "What have you done?"

Turning to face Adam, she lifted her eyes and chin and spoke directly to him. She saw the fierce strain etched into his strong face and she gave voice to the thoughts that fought one another to escape her mouth.

"Ish, how can this be?" she spoke slowly. Her words dripping in wonderment tinged with excitement and discouragement.

"Father said I would die if I touched the fruit but ..." She took a breath and let her words create a trail until the sound died in the air.

Her words started again but stronger this time. "Father said I would surely die if I ate the fruit ... but I'm right here ... speaking with you." Disbelief in the reality of the moment incapacitated them both.

Adam, matching her intelligence, had already understood this. He had only been two steps away from her when he watched her disobey a direct command from the Father. He had felt deep fear for the first time as he saw her rebel against God, but—and this was the part

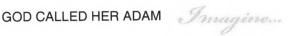

that left him in utter disbelief—*there she stood right here before him* as if the serpent's words were true and God's were not.

They both stared at the desirous fruit she still held in her hand. Seconds passed.

Emboldened, Woman twisted her hand slightly, relaxed her grasp on the fruit, and her delicate God-crafted fingers let it roll into her palm. She stretched out her arm so her hand moved toward Adam.

Adam looked down at the fruit and then back at Woman. It just didn't make sense. The Father was the giver of good gifts.

A cool breeze caught his attention as the Holy Spirit made a final appeal to Adam's heart.

In response, Adam shook his head repeatedly, as if saying no, and took a small step backward and said, "God said we are not to eat of the tree or ..." His words caught in his throat.

"Or we will surely die?" She finished the sentence for him as if it were a question, only now starting to feel the effects of something indescribable changing deep inside her.

Stunned, Adam faced what he had been unsuccessfully trying to reconcile.

As was his custom to do everything wholeheartedly, his heart flung open the door of doubt, giving permission for the demons to enter.

As Adam turned from the heart of God, the evil spirit called Disappointment divided his hold on Woman to reach for Adam. Disappointment accosted Adam as he took the fruit from her hand. Eyeing the wide-open door of doubt, Despair lunged for the great man of God and clung to Adam's unprotected flesh, pouring darkness into his heart.

How could Father have been so wrong? Adam thought in utter despair.

He put the remaining portion of the beautiful fruit in his mouth, chewed once, twice, and then swallowed.

The Aftermath

Even before the fruit entered his belly, the world Adam and Woman had known before was changed beyond their comprehension.

The standard raised by Holy Spirit fell hard as the demons swarmed in to inspect the creation that had been passed on to them by those who had been given dominion.

As the presence of those of darkness invaded Eden and earth, the creation began to die, seeing as it was now separated from God's glory. Death, the newest member of the demonic forces, strengthened its hold on earth and instantly became a high commander in the eyes of even matured fallen powers.

Death reveled in this unsought and unrivaled power over creation. He could end the abundant life given to the created, and He answered only to the one other evil force that had masterminded the overthrow played out in the garden: Satan.

The fruit traveled unhurriedly down Adam's throat but the minds of the man and woman crackled with fear as their world diminished in front of their eyes.

Unbeknown to them, their agreement to defy the living God's command and to align with the evil one cost them their God-granted dominion. Dominion had been granted to them; thus, Satan needed them both, man and woman, to pledge their authority over creation to him. Once this had been accomplished, Satan began to set up his reign on earth. The planet groaned under the weight of the shift but it was helpless to do anything other than accept the shift and bear it.

Ish and Isha looked skyward. The heavens seemed less brilliant, although the sky was still a beautiful blue hue. They noticed the sounds of the heavenly hosts were diminishing. What had been a continual soothing chorus of praise toward God was fast becoming voices heard more from memory or habit than with their ears.

While the heavenly voices drifted into whispers before fading into nothingness, the sounds of earth increased in volume and character. The roar of the lion, which had previously signaled a time to take a break from working to rest against the mighty creature's mane, created a surge of fear inside Adam. The roar now seemed like it was a challenge to Ish. He felt a need to defend his dominance. This was new.

Isha noticed the change in the ground itself. The soil that had clung to her feet because of the moisture therein was becoming "less." Unsure how to describe it, she remained silent.

Her gaze bumped and crashed across their home, their paradise, their Eden and she took in the first subtle changes. The leaves were not so full, the ground less moist. The birds still chattered in the trees but with a tinge of chaos.

There was something new here. Something much less than good and something outside of good. This something was moving across their garden like a fog, transforming the good that was present into the "less."

A bee buzzed past her face. She moved her hand to prod it to another path and it landed on her finger ... and stung her!

Stunned at the unexpected attack, she uttered a muted yelp and stumbled back a few steps, bumping into Adam who stood with eyes wide and mouth slightly ajar. He looked at her, at her finger and then back at their diminishing surroundings. It was only then that they started to understand that they had unleashed something beyond their understanding. Still they had no idea of the evil they had loosed on God's plan. They didn't understand that their actions had doomed themselves and their progeny to the hands of Death.

Taking a few quick steps from Adam and settling a few shoulder spans away, Woman put her stung finger in her mouth and nursed the wound until the stinger lifted to the surface. As she consoled herself, she stared at Adam's changed body and noticed that his penis was smaller than it had been before he ate the fruit. She took in the rest of his body. Something was different about his entire countenance, but what was it?

Adam noticed the area of the garden they had cultivated the evening before looked "less." But that wasn't possible given its appearance mere minutes before. He looked at Woman packing dirt on her swollen finger and ... crying?

He started toward her and noticed the tenderness of his feet against the hardening earth.

"Isha, what's happening? What have we done?" he spoke the words without malice but also without emotion. The words were not truly directed at Isha but were merely his way of thinking aloud.

Stopping just before reaching her, his mind took in the deadening of their dominion. Wrestling with his powerlessness to resist or even to predict the lessening of creation's glory, his eyes took in Isha. He noticed her breasts were alluring although somehow less. Her arms and legs seemed to be the same physically but something was different. Wrong. That special "knittedness" between them, that link, was "less."

As his concentration focused on her, she joined him in the visual inspection of her body. She recognized that she was smaller somehow although she was the same. She winced at the throbbing pain in her finger from the bee sting as she stood so both of them could finish their inspection.

He examined her from head to toes. She was still desirable, his bodily reaction made that undeniable, but even so she was "less" than before they had eaten the fruit.

Never considering examining himself, he spoke again. "Woman, what have you done? Look at you, the fruit has changed you."

Initially shocked, she reacted within seconds. Shifting her weight on her feet, she retorted, "Look at you. You have become less before my eyes."

At her words, Adam set his jaw and gazed down at himself. His skin seemed to cling more closely to his muscles and his penis was … different.

With a grating and ruthless clarity, they both knew their disobedience was having an effect on all they had ever known. Their disobedience was affecting the creation and their own bodies.

The memory of life before the fruit was in the forefront of their minds. The stark contrast of their bodies before and the bodies they possessed now caused them great shame. They were ashamed at their disobedience and ashamed they had brought this "lessening" into themselves.

They looked at each other with a once familiar understanding. Without words, they agreed to cover the evidence of their disobedience. They would cover their shame. They would begin by covering their bodies. They walked toward the fig trees.

Chapter 6

The Judgment

Although we commonly call the findings of God toward humankind after the fall "the curse," if you read the Scripture for what is says, it becomes clear that God is not cursing those created in His image. God curses the serpent and the ground, but He pronounces a judgement on those He loves who are now separated from Him. Given this important distinction, I prefer the word *"judgment"* over the word *"curse"* moving forward to describe the consequence of their disobedience.

Although given by a loving God, these judgments are just that, judgments.

> 14 Then the Lord God said to the serpent; Because you have done this, you are cursed more than any livestock and more than any wild animal. You will move on your belly and eat dust all the days of your life.
>
> 15 I will put hostility between you and the woman, and between your seed and her seed. He will strike your head, and you will strike his heel.
>
> 16 He said to the woman: I will intensify your labor pains; you will bear children in anguish. Your desire will be for your husband, yet he will rule over you.

17 And He said to Adam, "Because you listened to your wife's voice and ate from the tree about which I commanded you, 'Do not eat from it." The ground is cursed because of you. You will eat from it by means of painful labor all the days of your life. 18 It will produce thorns and thistles for you, and you will eat the plants of the field. 19 You will eat breads by the sweat of your brow until you return to the ground, since you were taken from it.

For you are dust, and you will return to dust. (Gen 3:14–19, HCSB)

Reading God's judgments as written, there are three parts that God spoke to Woman: 1) the hardship of pregnancy and the pain of labor, 2) the longing for a man, and 3) his dominion over her.

Pain

Interestingly, the increase in labor pain infers that, even in paradise, humanity could feel pain. God doesn't say He will give her pain; rather, He says he will *increase* her pain.

16 He said to the woman: I will intensify your labor pains; you will bear children in anguish. (Gen 3:16a, HCSB)

When God tells Woman about the exceeding pain, He chooses words that describe a pain that will descend on her like a swarm of locusts. We know she understands because she doesn't say, "Excuse me. Would you please define pain?"

The fact that she understands what pain is uncovers another assumption we may have made about what life in the "good" looks like. What does this mean if suddenly we understand that pain may actually have a rightful place in our lives?

Imagine that even in the Garden of Eden, Adam and Woman could remain in perfect communion with God and yet still fall out of a tree, bump their heads on a low-hanging bough, or endure any other manner of pain-causing accident. Can you see how Woman's understanding of pain implies she had a knowledge of pain?

I can imagine Adam and Woman deep in the foliage searching for their next ideas for the garden when Adam decides to get a better vantage point by climbing the closest tall tree. Adam begins climbing as he was likely used to doing but a little more than halfway to his goal, he gets careless and loses his grip on a branch. Once he lands on the ground, does he feel pain? I think this verse says he does. He felt pain and, although no fall could cause death, it could cause him pain. This experience would also remind him to be more careful on his next climb.

So, let's transfer the same to Woman. She can feel pain, but now God says, "You ain't seen nuthin' yet." The pain is all encompassing.

This hardship and swarming pain serves as a tribute to the day of the disobedience. It is with the fulfilling of the command to be fruitful that women, from the judgment forward, memorialize the destruction caused by the disobedience.

It is with stretch marks and muscle aches, all-consuming contractions and the crowning burn that each woman pays tribute to the first woman's portion in the transition of stewardship from those of God to those oppose Him.

The Longing …

Have you ever taken a moment to consider how having desire toward your husband is a judgment?

> and toward thy husband is thy desire, and
> he doth rule over thee. (Gen 3:16b, YLT)

I asked several women this question. One said it was because the woman was now going to desire to control the man. Other women were puzzled having never considered this Scripture very deeply.

I asked some men the same question: "How is a woman's desire toward her husband a judgment?" Most of those men, husbands and fathers, said because the woman would try to be the leader or control the household. Interestingly enough, only a few men seemed puzzled by the question.

Here is an opportunity for innocent bias. This Hebrew Scripture was being read and translated by men.

Can you imagine what those poor married men translating the Hebrew text were thinking as they read that God pointing Woman's desire toward man was a judgment?

It is important to understand that these men were translating the Hebrew text so it would make sense to the reader. They were not evil or even mischievous. Translation of the Holy Scripture was taken very seriously. People dedicated their entire lives to this sacred task.

So, return to the man translating this verse. He must translate it so it is understandable to his readers, who are also male, in a male-dominated society. This is our starting point.

At the time the Scriptures were first recorded, women were valued above chattel, but barely. It is easy to imagine that the men performing the translation could not understand how a woman's longing for a husband could be a judgment. But, as a testament to their integrity, they translated the Hebrew to the best of their ability even though it made little sense.

Now, in scouring the Bible for the truth to document in this book, an interesting set of facts surfaced regarding how the words of this verse are translated.

Let's use Young's Literal Translation for this important verse.

> and toward thy husband [is] thy desire, and
> he doth rule over thee. (Gen 3:16b)

Translators added the word *is* so the text would make sense to the English readers.

So, let's remove "is" since it is not present in the Hebrew:

and toward thy husband thy desire, and he
doth rule over thee.

What is extraordinarily interesting is the Hebrew word that is translated as "husband." This word is transliterated as "*ish*." Of the 1,639 times it is used in the Old Testament, it is translated as a word other than husband the majority of the time. This word "*ish*" is translated "husband" only sixty-nine times in the entire Old Testament. Once you see how it is translated the majority of the time, God's judgment will immediately become clear to most women. The most common translation of *ish* is "man." It is translated as man 1,002 times.

Now, we are really close to the truth. Remove "thy" because it only makes sense if you mistranslate the word *ish* as husband.

A final consideration is this: the word that comes directly before *ish* is the preposition "el." This word appears thirty-eight times in the Old Testament and is defined by Strong's as "to, into, towards." According to the Brown-Driver-Briggs Hebrew lexicon, as a preposition, it means *directed* or *disposed towards*.

So, removing the cultural bias and relying solely on the Hebrew, here is the Scripture restated using the preposition *el* and most common translation of the Hebrew word we know as *ish*:

'... and toward man thy desire, and he doth
rule over thee.

Using this appropriately translated verse, I asked the following question to men: How could a woman's desire toward man be a judgment? The reaction this time was for most men to correct me. These men redirected me and restated the verse to use "husband" rather than "man." Once I required the men to think about this Scripture using the word "man" rather than "husband", most of them were puzzled.

Then I asked women the same question: How is a woman's desire toward man a judgment?

Once asked this question, 100 percent of the women had a "light bulb" moment. Each woman clearly understood how desire toward a man rather than a husband was a judgment.

Women can tell many stories about themselves or other women where a woman, desiring a man, crashed off the path of righteousness or rationality. Yes, beloved, women *know* how desiring man can be a judgment.

This "desire" for a man has been interpreted in some Bible translations as "control." Meaning, the woman will want to usurp the man's role. She will want to dominate him. Two things strike me as strange here. Firstly, God's word choice, "desire" is literally "a longing for" as used in Song of Solomon where the fiancé is longing for his love to be available to him. Secondly, this thought assumes that man was in a superior position in the garden. If the woman wanted to usurp his role, it included the idea that the man has a superior role that the woman would want to attain. I think scriptural evidence for this, in the garden, is lacking.

We should allow God's word to speak for itself without our cultural biases interfering. This is difficult to do given the many presumptions made throughout history and in our multi-faceted Christian community and traditions.

At the time Moses captured God's words of creation in Genesis, humanity had a history spanning thousands of years. Traditions were in place. The Jewish people had passed the stories of the covenant with Abraham to their children for generations, through times of war and peace, in tribal times, as well as an evolution into a clan of people.

But God is faithful to transmit His word to us as purposed. God's word does not return void. And, in keeping with that truth, our challenge once again is to examine His word for what it actually says rather than what we interpret it to say.

His word says, "Woman: your desire will be for a man."

Simply put, a woman, under the judgment, will long for a man. She will feel compelled to have one. She will feel incomplete without one.

His Dominion Over Her

Another significant item is that this judgment meant that God was making a change from his original order. God's judgment was a change from the structure prior to the disobedience to the structure after the disobedience. The judgment is the point of change.

In the beginning, God created them male and female.

> 28 God blessed them; and God said to them, "Be fruitful and multiply, and fill the earth, and subdue it; and rule over the fish of the sea and over the birds of the sky and over every living thing that moves on the earth." (Gen 1:28, NASB)

Do you remember this verse? God told *them* that they were supposed rule over the creation. There is no mention of either of them ruling over the other.

And then the effect of the judgment was predicted: "he shall rule over thee." God is saying that this longing puts woman in a position that leads to a man ruling over her.

This is obviously a negative consequence directly related to the woman's desire for a man. So, why are Christians encouraging women remain subject to the consequence and to take subservient positions to men in their daily Christian lives?

If we trust that what God calls a judgment is truly a judgment, then we have to believe that a man ruling over a woman is to be detested. Yet, many times, in our Christian community, it is taught as God's will.

Understanding that this judgment was a change from God's original intention for the relationship between Adam and Woman, you see that this judgment of a man dominating a woman affects the man too. Whereas before the disobedience, they ruled equally and jointly, now, man will work to enlarge himself to overshadow and rule her.

The Hebrew word for dominion or to dominate is *mashal*. It means "to rule, reign, have dominion over."

God is clear. The time of parity was over. Not solely due to a radical change in the behavior of Woman but also due to the effect of sin in the heart of Adam toward her.

Chavvah, Eve

Judgment was pronounced over both Adam and Woman.

These judgments were leveled by a God who loves us as His children. These judgments were for our good.

With humanity being made in God's image, Adam and Woman could be an indomitable force for evil now that they had fallen. If they could remain unified, they could continue to cause both intentional and unintentional harm to themselves and the now groaning creation. We see this when humanity managed to join together to attempt to construct the tower of Babel.

> At one time the whole earth had the same language and vocabulary. 2 As people migrated from the east,[c] they found a valley in the land of Shinar and settled there. 3 They said to each other, "Come, let us make oven-fired bricks." They used brick for stone and asphalt for mortar. 4 And they said, "Come, let us build ourselves a city and a tower with its top in the sky. Let us make a name for ourselves; otherwise, we will be scattered over the face of the whole earth." (Gen 11:1–4, HCSB)

Humanity organized countries and cultures that were an affront to God's nature but as long as a remnant remained, God's plan soldiered forward toward redemption for that same humanity.

The Israelites did what was evil in the Lord's sight; they forgot the Lord their God and worshiped the Baals and the Asherahs. (Judges 3:7, NASB)

The Israelites again did what was evil in the sight of the Lord after Ehud had died. (Judges 4:1, NASB)

Now the sons of Israel again did evil in the sight of the Lord, so that the Lord gave them into the hands of the Philistines forty years. (Judges 13:1, NASB)

I think God needed to slow humanity down. He needed to occupy or divert our attention long enough to allow the institution of the covenant, and the voices of the prophets and then the victorious entry and sacrifice of His Son. These hardships; judgments did just that for us.

What an interesting statement made by Adam at the conclusion of God's judgment against humanity, Adam's next action was to change the name of his wife from "Woman," taken out of man, to Eve, "the mother of all living."

20 Now the man called his wife's name Eve, because she was the mother of all the living. (Gen 3:20, NASB)

Imagine what could have brought Adam to rightfully declare the gift of life to be borne by Eve when he, Adam, was now tasting death for the first time.

Let's join them for the final time as life as they had known it ends ...
Imagine ...

Judgment

Clad in fig leaves and shame, for them, morning came much quicker than either of them wanted.

As was the Father's habit, the cool wind of Holy Spirit cleared the way for Him as He entered Eden. Knowing what the couple had done, God's heart ran to greet them, calling for them.

"Where are you?"

God asked this question as He turned His back to the grove of trees where Ish and Isha attempted to conceal themselves from Him.

His love carried His voice to the ears of the created ones but, as His love reached them, a demon of Condemnation blocked their view and bound them in invisible chains.

Knowing of their willing turn against Him, God chose His words carefully. He wanted Adam and Woman to understand that He was well aware they were no longer free in the spirit. Knowing that they hardly had any comprehension of the devastation they had unleashed, God wanted them to recognize that His love for them had not changed. He wanted them to return to Him, but they would not yet allow themselves to be comforted. They had fallen from their ability to discern and command the spiritual realm. They had fallen into mere humanity. He understood the depth of that fall more than they did, now or forever.

The question "Where are you?" was the opening volley to allow either of them to show themselves in the flesh now that they were only that – dying flesh and separated spirit. But Adam and Woman remained hidden.

God allowed some time to pass before He approached the grove of trees in which they had hidden themselves.

Clinging to each other, Woman nodded to Adam as though he should be the first to expose himself to the Father. In silence, he agreed. He suckled a morsel of pride that was being fed to him by the demon of Contempt. Swallowing, Adam stood and steadied himself.

"I," Adam said as he stepped out into the openness in view of God, "I heard your voice and was afraid." He lowered his head,

glancing back at Isha to remember the reason he had stepped out of the shadows.

"I was afraid because I was naked, so I hid myself." After freeing the words out of the trap that was his body, Adam felt better, stronger. He straightened his spine a bit and stood taller but still couldn't bring himself to look at God's face.

God, blessed to hear Adam's honest confession, felt His heart tearing because He loved him deeply. Yet God knew He had to save Adam by issuing a judgment Adam couldn't possibly understand at that moment.

God moved slowly toward Adam while keeping their eyes connected. Holy Spirit swept around Adam attempting to soothe him in the presence of the evil trying to influence him but, by then, his awareness of the spiritual had been nearly depleted. He could not hear and could scarcely detect Holy Spirit's presence.

Close enough for Adam to touch Him, God turned His eyes to the place in the shadows where Isha still hid. The edges of His mouth turned up slightly like a smile as His thoughts enjoyed the memory of her eyes the moment she loved Him for the first time.

Her *ra'ah*, her ability to see and perceive deeply, was greatly diminished. Her ability to discern the immaterial remained intact, although it was a shadow of its former greatness. Recognizing the Father's love, she walked toward God, following the trail that His love provided back to its source, albeit with her head and eyes downcast.

They both stood in the presence of the almighty God. That day, they stood in the love of the one they called Father. Standing here, their shame multiplied and they shifted in their wretched fig leaves.

The Holy One bent down on one knee to the level of Adam. He wanted Adam to look at Him, but the weight of the shame was heavier than even the mighty man could resist.

In a way that He would later do on the cross, the Word reached out to Adam and lifted his chin, bearing the weight of Adam's shame.

Looking deeply into Adam's spiritually dull eyes, God created a way for Adam to release the plague of condemnation for doubting the intention of the One who loved him beyond comprehension.

God asked Adam the question forcefully but in a way not to increase his fear, "Who told you you were naked?"

At the question, the events of "the lessening" pillaged Adam's mind. The memories of colors dimming, animals whining and roaring, their own bodies changing and their minds ... their minds were different. Their minds swatted at thoughts that seemed not to be of them, although some of those not-good-thoughts were slowly bubbling up from Adam's spirit as it died to God's glory.

Adam knew eating the fruit had opened their eyes to evil. He saw and was experiencing the "less than good."

Interrupting the silence, God continued gently, "Did you eat from that tree I told you not to eat from?"

At the question, fear found its way past pride and repentance. Adam turned and did what he never imagined he could do. He turned toward the woman he loved and, looking at her rather than God, said, "The woman you gave me as a companion gave me fruit from the tree, and, yes, I ate it."

Woman experienced a storm of emotions with his proclamation of the truth. Shock because he offered her instead of himself out of fear. Anger because she felt betrayed, although they shared that trait that day. Resignation because the words were true. Her face belied the storm of thoughts and emotions raging inside her now mortal flesh, and she stood ... silent and accused.

Turning to face her fully and understanding her wrestling with these waves of chaos influenced by emotional pain, God whispered in her direction, offering her the same chance to wash her mind by confessing, "Woman, what have you done?"

Seeing no way out, she sputtered the pathetic and pitiful truth. "The serpent seduced me, and I ate the fruit."

She started crying out of her pain for the second time since her creation; the second time since eating the fruit. Unbidden tears and saliva mixed as they dripped from her face and left slow-moving trails across her covering of fig leaves.

Her grief overtook her. She stepped forward with her arms open wide in an effort to be held by the Father's loving arms. She brought her hands together to cling to His neck, intending to bury her head

in His chest, but her body found no barrier to stop her tumble forward to the still somewhat soft ground. Her mortal flesh, her dying, fruit-consuming, fallen body could no longer commune with the Spirit of God. It passed right through the Eternal One's fading visage.

She lay on the ground sobbing uncontrollably as she grieved the enormity of her loss of intimate communion with the One she now knew had given her everything good and held nothing back.

God's heart lay tattered beside her as she heaved on the ground in despair.

God rose up as judge. He stood to penalize the ones who had come against His beloved - to protect them from the full penalty of their wrong.

Seeing the serpent frozen in an alerted state, clinging to the lowest bough of the adjacent tree, God cursed the serpent to an unchangeable future:

"Because you've done this, you're cursed, cursed beyond all cattle and wild animals. Cursed to slink on your belly and eat dirt until you die. I'm declaring war between you and the Woman, between your offspring and hers. He'll wound your head, you'll wound his heel."

Having already lost the ability to speak due to the effect of the change of dominion, the serpent withered until it remained on its belly and had a deep desire for dirt.

The meaning of the remaining portion of the curse was lost on the serpent but not on the host of evil forces that were arranged just outside the area illuminated by God's brilliance. They understood that God was about to wage a war they could not win but even they lacked full understanding of the mystery God released in the curse.

God turned to Woman who, by this time, was consoled by Adam to the best of his ability. As Adam helped her to her feet, she looked at what little she still saw of the One she loved and she waited. Tears welled in her eyes again, although she wondered how she could have more tears to cry.

She rested some of her weight onto Adam and braced herself for the punishment she knew she deserved.

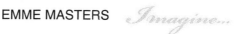

God managed a smile even though He knew she was too overwhelmed to understand the fence of life that His judgment would create for her sake and the sake of their descendants.

"Woman," the Father paused and held her gaze until she could find and focus on His love.

"I'll multiply your pains in childbirth. You'll give birth to your babies in pain. You'll want to please your man, but he'll lord it over you."

She collapsed against Adam in relief. She was so grateful to the Father! He had shown His mercy once again. She would live and not die. She would have babies! God would allow her another chance to fulfill His command to be fruitful.

The judgment of death from eating the fruit was not coming by the Father's hand, but she knew death would still come. Now, her trust in God's words could never be shaken.

Adam provided support for the still trembling woman as she struggled to stand without his assistance. He recognized and respected God. If this human body could have contained it, Adam's genuine admiration would have made him gleam with radiance as in times past, but this body could not. Even more unsettling, he felt their deeper connection waning. Having seen the destruction their disobedience had caused and having seen God's merciful judgment for Woman, Adam watched God's mouth and waited for His next words.

God stood in front of Adam and out of His kindness selected the judgement that would keep his hands busy and his mind occupied for centuries to come.

"Because you listened to your wife and ate from the tree that I commanded you not to eat from, the very ground is cursed because of you. Getting food from the ground will be as painful as having babies is for your wife. You'll be working in pain throughout your life. The ground will sprout thorns and weeds, you'll get your food the hard way, planting and tilling and harvesting, sweating in the fields from dawn to dusk, until you return to that ground yourself, dead and buried. You started out as dirt, you'll end up dirt."

Adam and Woman, who had believed they would receive death as due recompense for their eating of the fruit, saw His words of judgment as life and a future.

They saw each judgment contained talk of babies and a future. That meant they would live.

Adam, vowing in his mind to unflinchingly follow God's commands for the rest of his days, held Woman tightly in his arms. He knew how much more she wanted to be held by their father but, he would hold her until she could be held by the Holy One again.

Adam loved Woman deeply.

She stood a little straighter to pull out of his arms enough to look at him. She wanted to see his face, to read his expression, to see if she still "pleased him."

He returned her gaze and she knew. She *ra'ah*.

Looking at her, he loved her and, in a declaration of who she would become according to God's judgment, Adam said, "Isha, from now forward you will be Chavvah, Eve, because you are life."

She understood his proclamation of their future. Chavvah, or Eve, understood that through her life-giving body they would be fruitful and multiply.

She returned his gaze without reservation and she loved him back.

She had no understanding of how the man who held her so lovingly in his arms could ever find it in his heart to "lord over her," but this experience had taught her that her Creator's words were always true and never to be doubted. A quiet sob caught in her throat as she anticipated the heartache that was to come. Eve would only catch rare glimpses of Adam lording over her in their life together. It would take only a few generations for this judgment to fully blossom in their heirs.

The fig leaves scratched against their skin, leaving an ever-growing number of small scrapes and irritations on the fruit-wrenched bodies. Knowing the time was short before they became totally separated spiritually from His presence, God performed one of the final acts of kindness for his beloved Adam and Eve. God made them clothes of soft, supple leather and took precious moments to dress them with His own hands.

God also made sure to heal their wounds as He dressed them. In the minutes before their ears became as deaf to Him as their eyes were becoming blind to Him, He kissed them and loved them as only He could.

With His eyes still on them, He spoke aloud, although they could no longer hear His voice with distinction. His heart remained with them. God looked at their surroundings and took in the encroaching presence of the ones that had evil intentions for these— His beloved. They were waiting for the Lord's glory to fully fade from the presence of Adam and Eve.

"Humanity has become like one of us, capable of knowing everything, ranging from good to evil."

God said, "What if they now should reach out and take fruit from the Tree-of-Life and eat, and live forever? Never—this cannot happen!"

God shook His head, emphasizing that He would not allow them to live eternally in this condition so far beneath their intended reign. Appreciating their vulnerability to the influences of the new prince of the world, God stretched out before them to protect them.

Recognizing their unflinching allegiance to Him in the fullness of their meager, warring, mortal flesh; God erected a definitive hedge of protection, "Eden can no longer be your home." He said, "You must leave this place and begin your lives as mere humans, tilling the ground from which you were made."

This made no sense to them but, having learned that God was faithful to them even when faced with their faithlessness and doubt, they set about gathering their tools and other necessities for the next chapter of their existence.

And then … at least in their eyes, He was gone and they were alone for the first time in the chaos of the garden without the tangible presence of God.

Adam and Eve had lived only in the knowledge of good until they disobeyed God with the tree and its fruit. It was in that moment, having lost the ability to freely commune with God's creation and with the Creator, they took another giant leap forward in their

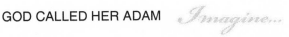

understanding of the devastation wrought by their folly. They were growing in the knowledge of that which was not "good."

Leaving the garden, they continued their trek into the knowledge of evil.

After their exit, God stationed a warrior angel with a revolving sword of fire to guard the path to the Tree of Life.

God would now begin His plan of redemption. He would not allow them (and us) to remain captive. God planned to sacrifice everything to restore us to His presence.

The battle for the souls of humanity had begun.

Chapter 7

Eve: Judgment Bound

Have you thought about the challenges Eve faced upon leaving the garden? What are the differences for women between the time of judgment in the garden of Eden and today? Not many of us have given much thought to the impact of the judgment on our lives, but this is an important discussion to have because it has shaped and is shaping the way we live.

From the time Adam and Eve exited the garden until now, men, and eventually women, have kept Eve imprisoned in the garden judgment.

After more than ten thousand years of human history, most Christians consider it a "fact" that a man should rule over a woman. This concept is so engrained in our Christian culture, that many women have been taught and are teaching younger women and new Christian sisters how to be ruled. This should not be so.

When created, God called her Adam. When introduced to Adam, man called her Woman. Immediately following the judgment in Eden, man changed her name to Eve.

Revisit the path of the female creation.

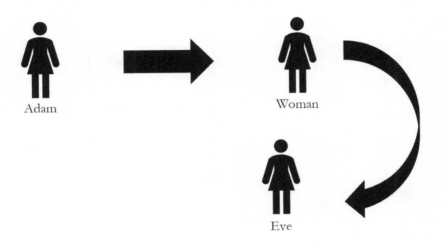

> Now the man called his wife's name Eve, because she was the mother of all the living. (Gen 3:20, NASB)

This transition is important to keep in your mind. Before the fall and before she was Eve, she fulfilled two roles one at a time: one as Adam—the single, talented, and powerful one—and the other as Woman, the powerful ally, the equal counterpart to Adam.

In the last section of this book, we watched Adam and Eve exit Eden to begin a new life in spiritual death. We know from biblical history that they went on to have children and the Bible gives us various levels of detail about some of their children's lives.

In reading the Old testament, we can see changes in culture and community. Over time, we see documentation of the judgment's impact. In the garden, Adam did not dominate Woman, but by the time of Abraham, women were being dominated as a matter of course—not only by their husbands but men in general.

Remember that several ideas were put forth in the Eden judgment. I have presented a chart for easy reference. This chart lists the curses and judgments, if we routinely overcome the judgment and the means by which the judgment can be overcome. A tickmark is placed in the column to identify the means by which the judgment can be overcome.

Curse or Judgment	Has it been overcome? (Yes/No)	The Will of Man – Natural Activity	The Will of God – Spiritual Activity
Serpent crawls on its belly	No	NA	NA
Seed of the woman crush his head …	Yes		✔
Childbirth is troubled and painful	Yes	✔	
The Woman longs for a man, and the Man dominates her	No (and Yes)		✔
The ground is cursed	Yes	✔	
Man works "By the sweat of his brow" to produce food	Yes	✔	

We will ignore judgment against the serpent's body and only discuss the judgments as they impact humanity.

> ➢ The woman shall have trouble in childbirth and pain in delivery. These judgments affected the physical body and are easy to understand. In an earlier time, the mortality rate of women related to childbirth was very high. These judgments affected Eve and her female progeny but did not create any subtle or imperceptible

effects. Women experience pregnancy and childbirth a few times in their lives or not at all. This judgment does not impact every woman—only women who become pregnant. The curse of the ground resulted in a judgment against Adam, causing him to toil to make the ground produce. It had more than a superficial impact. This judgment meant that Adam, in his fallen mortal flesh, would experience fatigue, frustration and a full range of emotions as it related to cultivating the soil.

➤ We will spend time examining two more judgments: the judgment of Woman longing for a man and the man dominating her. Ultimately, we will see how these judgments relate to God's redemption plan described by the serpent's seed and the seed of the woman in Genesis 3:15.

Between the Eden judgment and now, humanity has worked to ease the impact of the judgments. Think about the trouble of childbirth for women. With various techniques and medications, a woman in a developed country can expect a relatively painless childbirth experience from conception to delivery.

The ability to walk into a grocery store and purchase food without having to spend time in the fields sowing seeds or harvesting is a testament to how far humanity has distanced itself from hard physical labor to eat. While it remains true for most that some sort of exchange of labor for currency is required to buy the "fruit of the ground," it is not the "sweat of the brow" that was pronounced against Adam in the Eden judgment.

What I find very interesting is that humanity has worked hard to reverse the effects of the Eden judgment, except in a single instance: the judgment against Woman as it relates to "the longing" and to man dominating her. These judgments have not only been ignored, they have been perpetuated century after century and are only recently being reexamined.

We will examine the consequence of humanity's choice to accept and even profligate her longing for a man and domination of women.

Let's look at how this longing and domination by man has become a part of our expectations and then review God's word for direction toward redemption and restoration of his daughters so they will long for God rather than a man.

We will do it for one of the most important emotions impacted by "the longing": love.

Love and the Longing

Love and the search for it is the impetus for many stories told and retold at family events. We have all heard of the romantic, or not so romantic, tales of how our grandparents met and married. Most of us have heard the story of how our parents met so many times we could recite the story in our sleep!

What is it about these stories that draw us? Love and the thought of it brings smiles to most faces when we think of the positive effects in our lives and the lives of those we care about.

Love is worth the chase. Love is worth sacrifice. However, love, or what we call love, can have a critically negative impact on women when managed outside of God's guidance.

What does the Bible say about love?

God has granted us total freedom within His safe harbor. Should we use God's wisdom when we think or act on love? Would our lives be better or worse if women fastened themselves to God? How does living as God describes impact "the longing" of the judgment? These are important questions.

In this chapter, we will address some of the concepts about love that are contrary to God's instructions. Without your awareness, these ideas may have crept into your library of ideas. We will release these contradictory ideas from the lie to which they are attached. Once exposed, we can bind our renewed ideas to their rightful place in God's love for us. We will examine our ideas about love that ignore God's warnings and feed "the longing." Some have misconstrued the value of the longing by painting it as an ideal. Let me be clear, the longing is not a treasure but a thief. Let's discuss if what we know of love today matches the love God intended.

Love As a Safe Space

What is a safe space? It is generally thought of as a place where you are not under threat, where no harm will come to the occupant.

But how did we arrive at the thought that love is a safe space? How did we reach a place where we justify our radically emotional, illogical or just plain "bad" behavior by saying we are "in love?" I suggest that *if* we abide by God's instructions to us, not only will we live a more satisfying life with love, we will also live in an *abundance* of love.

Let's start examining love as a safe space by confronting the idea that love is a sufficient foundation to build a strong relationship.

Not so long ago, I was on social media browsing posts. One post caught my attention and my heart. It was a post from an outrageously beautiful young woman. It turns out she was a single mom and was just starting to succeed financially. She was very nimble with posting and, from her photos, she looked like she was having a lot of carnal fun. I continued to view her photos and posts and that is when I saw the following heartbreaking post. I'm not sure I can quote it exactly but it was something close to: "I just want to be able to say 'I love you' to a man and not feel stupid."

Do you know someone who has spoken this aloud? Are you that person?

Let's examine love in light of the Bible.

"First comes love then comes marriage, then comes Jane with a baby carriage." This was a child's rhyme that my friends and I used to chant as young girls, teasing each other about some little boy we adored for the moment.

What happens when we use love rather than the absolute truths found in God's word as a foundation for our relationships or our decisions? Can we trust love to be a solid foundation? Is love enough to make us happy, to satisfy us and keep us safe?

> The heart is more deceitful than anything
> else, and incurable—who can understand it? (Jer
> 17:9, HCSB)

Deceitful means willing to act apart from the truth. It is precisely because the heart is deceitful, meaning the heart will trick you, that so many talented women build relationships on a foundation consisting of the feeling of love rather than chasing God and allowing God to let her enjoy the maturation of her skills and talents in her time as Adam.

> Love is patient; love is kind. Love does not
> envy; is not boastful; is not conceited; 5 does not
> act improperly; is not selfish; is not provoked;
> does not keep a record of wrongs; 6 finds no
> joy in unrighteousness, but rejoices in the truth;
> 7 bears all things, believes all things, hopes all
> things, endures all things. 8 Love never ends. (1
> Cor 13:4–8a, HCSB)

Think hard about the veracity of love described here.

Can you see how easy it is to confuse love with the Eden judgment of "longing for a man?" The longing makes women vulnerable to using the emotion of love to absolve themselves of the responsibility to remain true to integrity as defined by the Holy Bible.

Love, without covenant, can be very one-sided. This biblical description of love seems not to require anything from the one who receives the love. This biblical description of love only makes demands on the love itself from the person giving it.

When women place love above God's instructions for his daughters, they set up a scenario for disappointment and bitterness, especially when that love is given in a one-sided way and is not reciprocated. When a woman's love is manipulated and she gives either more of her mind or body in an unfortunate exchange to acquire what she thinks is love, women become a breeding ground for cynicism.

Outside of covenant or marriage, this emotion-based, nonbiblical love can be dangerous to a woman's emotional health. Without bounds, the love described here could describe the actions of victims of domestic abuse.

How many women do you know who have followed their emotions to heartbreak or destruction, being dragged behind the longing for a man and chasing after love? They have traded the redemption and wisdom of God's everlasting love for the feeling of love toward a man. Love or being in love, by itself, does not create the divine safe space for a woman's heart. In fact, love alone easily constructs a chamber of torture, unrest, discomfort and even abuse. Never confuse the love to or from a man to be equal to or even close to the love of God for you.

The description of love in 1 Corinthians is the love of God, our Father. We often abuse His love, yet His love is always toward us, even if it is heavily one-sided and unreciprocated from humanity.

Trust the love that God has for you. His love offers depth, purpose and a perception that fulfills women beyond their greatest longing. This fulfillment is the shield of protection for a woman's heart, soul and life.

This is God's heart and the reflection of *love*. Remember, God is love. God's love is the only safe space where a foundation of love can be trusted.

If you have built any part of your relationship with a man on a foundation structured outside of God's instructions for love, for you, love is not a safe space.

Love At First Sight

Some people say they are victims of love. These people claim to have been stricken by love at first sight. If this were true, how could they do anything other than succumb to having love, with or without God's instruction, as a foundation for their relationship?

We will begin by reviewing what is necessary to believe in love at first sight. Then we will reexamine our thoughts about this concept.

For love at first sight to be true, the emotion of "love" must be redefined. To say that anyone is capable of experiencing real, emotional love without knowledge of the other person is to strip away the inward parts of what defines love.

In the way it would be silly to say Tina delivered a bouncing teenager (instead of a newborn boy), certain impossibilities are denied at your peril.

The truth is love is a decision. Love is a commitment. It has an emotional component that feels dreamy but it is also substantial. It is deep-rooted and settled. Like a seed, love is hidden and reaches into the soul, putting down roots before reaching heavenward to take its first glimpse of sunshine and first taste of air.

But "the longing" incorporates elements other than love to draw women into the snare. Sometimes attraction is confused for love. Attraction can also be a very dangerous ingredient for the longing.

Sometimes one person feels attraction toward another person. At the same time, they can feel something familiar deep within; perhaps the person moves their hair or hands in the same way as a person they once knew and liked. When familiarity is coupled with attraction, it feels like love.

Be careful. This attraction must be handled carefully because it feels like you already know the person – but the truth is, you don't know the person at all.

Like a baby develops in its mother's womb, love needs a place to grow and develop. Or maybe love, like a baby, is born after the parents get to know each other, discover secrets and exchange moments. Attraction, even strong attraction, is not love.

For the person who believes in love at first sight, my question is this: In the first second that you saw the object of your "love," what about that person did you love?

The truth is knowing nothing of the object of your "love," you are only "loving" what you imagine about the person.

It is only after knowing the object of your "love" you can answer the question of "What is it that you love about this person?"

You cannot honestly love, in the true sense of what love means, until you know the person. You can only come to know a person after repeated genuine interactions and conversations. It is only when you know the person that you have the beginnings of what can be called love.

The Fruit of Living in Longing

How many women have set aside their dreams for the whims of a man? I am not speaking about a married couple who, together, decide to prioritize their lives. I am thinking of the young girl in high school who skips class to be with her boyfriend or disobey her parents to chase her "longing for a man." I am thinking of the young woman who is gifted in so many ways discontinuing a promising college education to satisfy her "longing for a man."

There is also the Christian woman whose "longing for a man" causes her to discard her reputation and integrity toward living as the Bible declares best and instead chooses to live outside of marriage with the man she loves.

To be clear, we are not speaking only of women and girls with painful histories or neglectful fathers or parents. This irrational longing is not only happening to kids from broken homes. This longing is defeating the role models for our youth.

This phenomenon of pairing up with a man, living with him outside of covenant, serial or long-term dating inclusive of sex was once framed as rebellious or wrong by society. It is now accepted as part of the journey along the path to adulthood. But is this truth?

There is a biological time when young people begin to notice each other. It used to be around puberty, which was mid to late teens. In the early twenty-first century, puberty has sprouted earlier and earlier, so now the average age is about ten years old.

This makes our girls particularly vulnerable. Although physical maturation is occurring at an earlier age, emotional maturation is moving in the opposite direction.

Women, think back to your first sexual encounter with a man. Anecdotally, I know of no woman who was wowed by the experience. Her spirit and brain had to take time to make these new physical and soulish connections. Her mind worked to incorporate what she had anticipated happening to what actually happened and finally to the present. These revelations were codified over the next hours and days. But, what it wasn't, was the anticipated enchantment.

And yet ... a sexual encounter triggers a spiritual pairing that is the proverbial ball and chain for the unmarried woman. This joining of souls is both real and merciless.

Sex and The Longing

To use the analogy of fishing, if attraction and the feeling of love is the lure of the longing; then sex is the hook.

The message that is pulsed daily through the media is that people, and women in particular, are not enough.

The point of this marketing mantra is to mold us into perfect consumers—consumers who are driven to become adequate, desirable and whole. But, the reality is that a redeemed woman is already whole and to rely on any material item is to exchange the foundation built on the identity God gave her for an identity built on ever-changing cultural trends which swing widely.

If women accept who they are in God, their gifts will turn this world right-side up. Their skills will bind families where they have sagged and their talents can become the resolve to behave and progress in unimaginable ways. Instead, this vulnerability of longing for a man has been exploited. Remember the subsequent consequence of the judgment of longing is that the man will dominate her.

If you will think back a few chapters, we discussed how the other Adam was made to be a functional opposite of the first. Neither of the Adams were lacking or needy. Both were matched in such a way that, although their skills and talents were not identical, their personhood was equal.

Once the longing was introduced, the way men and women related to each other shifted. Women were no longer functioning as equals - although, in reality, they were capable of functioning as equals. With the longing, women sought out a man's presence and comfort. Men did not have this longing; therefore, there was a power shift. Women felt as though they needed a man. With this change, men were able to dominate women. It simply required the acceptance of a woman's need.

The fact that men leveraged this need for their benefit is not a condemnation against men. The character of humanity is such that we tend to take advantage of situations that profit us. As an illustration, let's go back to the two children we met earlier, Campbell and Taylor.

Imagine that Campbell and Taylor are playing well together with their toys. A parent brings in a new toy for each child. Each child is happy to receive a new toy but Campbell, although happy with the toy, wants Taylor's toy. Once Taylor realizes Campbell's longing for the toy, Taylor can manipulate Campbell's actions. As long as Campbell wants Taylor's toy, Taylor can require Campbell to behave to Taylor's satisfaction to gain access to the toy.

This could mean Campbell has to give Taylor all Campbell's toys to play with in exchange for time to play with Taylor's toy. In the same way, over time, women's behavior was molded to men's ideals in exchange for male companionship. Eventually, this exchange ensured that women became restricted to a small portion of the world's opportunities.

Over time, as humanity moved further from God, men found themselves in an ever-tempting position to take advantage of the longing borne by the Eves of the world. Men came to dominate women, as women traded power to satisfy the need to consistently feed the longing for a man.

Men came to believe that women needed them due to a lack in themselves, conveniently forgetting God's judgment against women. Men systematically began to create rules and expectations for the woman's behavior. They understood well that women desired men to feel satisfied, but men, without this longing, sequestered women for sexual companionship and childbearing.

Over time, Christian women were cajoled into believing they were the servants of men. They believed their domain was only the home and wholeheartedly embraced the judgment of men ruling over them as if it was the truth as God intended. We know, by reading Scripture, that this was the judgment given after humanity's disobedience and before the redemption by our Savior Jesus.

By the twentieth century, women were only in the embryonic stages of understanding their equality in the secular landscape. Because subservience to men was so engrained in the Christian culture, many Christian women felt helpless to engage in the fight to express their talents in areas other than the home and other traditional areas reserved for women such as teaching and nursing. This had the unfortunate consequence of having one of the most important movements for women go forward without the leadership of Christians or strong Christian influences on the fore.

The misunderstanding of the rightful place of women according to God has required the silence of godly women while the world has claimed the relevant topics. The silence of these strong leaders is the reason the culture has omitted God's values when identifying equality. Because the definition of equality was crafted outside the mind of the Bible and the Church, the culture spends its existence trying to convince its young girls and women that equality means women should align with the behaviors of the powerful, who have been men. Once again, there is no reference to God's intentions.

In one of the earlier chapters, I asked you a question: Is the rule about sexual relationships the same for men and women? Earlier, you responded; now, we will let God respond.

> An overseer, then, must be above reproach, the husband of one wife (1 Tim 3:2a, NASB)
>
> Drink water from your own cistern and fresh water from your own well. (Prov 5:15, NASB)
>
> Let your fountain be blessed, and rejoice in the wife of your youth. 19 As a loving hind and a graceful doe, Let her breasts satisfy you at all times; Be exhilarated always with her love. (Prov 5:18–19, NASB)
>
> 25 Husbands, love your wives, just as Christ loved the church and gave Himself for her 26 to make her holy, cleansing her with the washing

of water by the word. 27 He did this to present the church to Himself in splendor, without spot or wrinkle or anything like that, but holy and blameless. 28 In the same way, husbands are to love their wives as their own bodies. He who loves his wife loves himself. 29 For no one ever hates his own flesh but provides and cares for it, just as Christ does for the church, 30 since we are members of His body. 31 For this reason a man will leave his father and mother and be joined to his wife, and the two will become one flesh. (Eph 5:25–31, HCSB)

When a man takes a new wife, he shall not go out with the army nor be charged with any duty; he shall be free at home one year and shall give happiness to his wife whom he has taken. (Deut 24:5, NASB)

But because sexual immorality is so common, each man should have his own wife, and each woman should have her own husband. 3 A husband should fulfill his marital responsibility to his wife, and likewise a wife to her husband. 4 A wife does not have the right over her own body, but her husband does. In the same way, a husband does not have the right over his own body, but his wife does. 5 Do not deprive one another sexually—except when you agree for a time, to devote yourselves to prayer. Then come together again; otherwise, Satan may tempt you because of your lack of self-control. (1 Cor 7:2–5, HCSB)

First Corinthians 7:2–5 is relevant and powerful for us today. This passage begins with "Because sexual immorality is so common." This is God clearly outlining the difference between sexual immorality and what He chooses for us.

In all the verses mentioned here, men are repeatedly prescribed one wife. Men are instructed to love her, satisfy her and find their satisfaction in her. But the Church's silence has allowed the secular culture to negate the importance of sexual morality. Because of sin, men did not satisfy themselves with one wife. Men had multiple wives. Men committed adultery so much so that it became an unwilling expectation for many wives whose husbands wielded power. In general, men behaved as ones with a fallen nature and the power to fulfill fleshly lusts.

In the search for equality, women have erroneously aligned themselves with the secular definition of equality. They have claimed their freedom by having multiple or uncommitted sexual partners. The incidence of adultery committed by wives, rather than by husbands, has reached an alarming rate. A growing number of women choose not to marry. This is not due to their devotion to our Father but rather, the consequences of accepting the new normal for the actions of women.

Accepting this ill-defined freedom, women have viewed modesty as a prison rather than a gift. Strong women of God remaining silent is the reason women are being taught (and believe) their sexuality should be indulged rather than reverenced and protected in marriage. Today, many of our young women laugh at the profane or disregard God's wisdom willfully or out of ignorance. Now that our daughters are absentmindedly sexual, the people of God have, belatedly, started to loudly protest by speaking against cultural norms that are impacting our women negatively. Christians are speaking publicly about behaviors that, in previous generations, were only spoken of privately, if at all. Christians are pulling together in love to raise awareness of the error and to uncover the lies that hurt our girls and women. Thankfully, it is not too late!

God's heart has remained true toward His daughters. His love, as described in His Word, has created a refuge for the hearts of women and sanctuary for their souls.

But we do not grieve as those who have no hope. Because we have Christ, who can redeem the time and give seed to the sower, the souls of our women can be retrieved and restored as long as God is allowed to rule.

Arousing the Lion

When the sexual revolution was in full swing in the 1960s, the advent of the birth control pill allowed women to be "free" from the threat of becoming pregnant. In the minds of people who did not have a relationship with the Lord, the reduced risk of pregnancy was equivalent to advocating sexual activity outside of marriage. It wasn't and it isn't.

Those without Jesus saw the pill as the gateway to disregard the wisdom of one lifetime sexual partner to advocating sex with only physical pleasure in mind.

They did not have biblical wisdom to alert them that humanity is diverse and consists of a physical body, emotions and thoughts (commonly called the soul) and spirit. They didn't consider the mind-boggling enormity of God's love and the path He carved for His beloved to avoid the unnecessary heartache during their time here on earth.

In their ignorance, they reveled seemingly without consequences. They made it look fun, so free. They washed the culture with their brand of love and Christian women looked on. Some were shocked but others were envious.

And, of course, there were consequences.

Women still had unintended pregnancies but now, because of the less rigorous standards applied to their male partners, the women may not have wanted a lifetime commitment. The other cultural shift was the lessening of cultural pressure for the man to commit to the woman because she was now free to choose life or death for her unborn child with the passage of Roe v. Wade. Increased pregnancies led to increased acceptance of single mothering. Men were fully benefitting from the sexual "freedom" of women. They had more access to sexual relationships with women without having to assume any responsibilities for the consequences.

Couple these changes with a skewed idea of equality and the "superwoman" was born. This "superwoman" worked outside the home, raised children acting as both mother and father and had an active sexual lifestyle. This woman didn't need a man, but she still wanted one. She was called superwoman, but in reality, women had simply returned to the exit of Eden, chaining themselves to the judgment of the longing of wanting a man although they were fully capable, with Christ, to be fulfilled without a man.

This cycle of bringing the modern woman back to the beginning of the days of judgment is the coalescing of the hunter becoming the hunted. Women were deceived once again. They believed the lie that equality and freedom rested in mimicking the level of sin in the lives of the powerful.

As marketing increased the use of sex to sell everything from cigarettes to bubble gum, the images being devoured by consumers became the images men craved and women aspired to become. Fast-forward fifty years and instead of innuendo, sexual acts are depicted on general TV in such a way as to make married women avert their eyes. The music that is most popular across many genres is filled with vivid details of sexual wishes and acts and these words can be heard from the mouths of babes over rhythm and beats that capture the listener. Casual conversation includes terms for women that, not long ago, would have caused women to come to blows. But in our day, we have tried to redefine them as terms of affection.

Now that women are experiencing sexual "freedom," their emotional suffering is skyrocketing. The deception was in convincing women that they thrive in the same sexual environment as men but it simply is not so.

God created women to connect the immaterial—that is simply what they do. Once God introduced the male Adam to the female Adam, Woman emerged. She connected with him on a soul level. Women make soul-level connections that are visible in the natural world. This talent is part of who she is. Women can engage this skill willingly, but the truth is, with the introduction of sex, these connections do not require her consent. This means she can't "not connect" by will. The default is to connect.

In Christianity, there is a concept of "soul ties." Many books have been written about this topic but for the purposes of our discussion we will say that the principle states that sex can create a spiritual or soul-level connection.

This concept of soul ties is not a solely Christian idea but many Christians accept it as truth. God knows this about women. It is His *love* that is written for us and cries to women to engage only in this bonding with their husband, the man with whom they will spend their life. This kind of bonding is dangerous for a woman if used recklessly. It is why so many women find themselves saying, "I want to say 'I love you' and not feel stupid."

Because Adam was created as a whole being and his existence did not always include the presence of a woman, many times men underestimate the nonsexual value women add. Sexual fulfillment is the one quantifiable experience that only women hold for him.

Here again we see how women, having believed that they can thrive in the same sexual environment as men, have tried to empower themselves by promoting their own sexuality as a means to gain power. This has resulted in the near impossibility of finding blouses and sweaters that do not expose cleavage or cling to the body. Female sprinters compete in scant clothing, while their male counterparts are nearly fully clothed albeit in spandex. Female superheroes are large breasted and show breast cleavage as well as butt cleavage. Female heroines nearly always have revealing costumes or exude sexuality. Women of intellectual importance are also portrayed in media in low-cut blouses and form-fitting clothing. Women are still being marketed the lie that power is primarily found in their bodies and they are still believing it.

Women need to be aware of their completeness so they never reduce themselves to a single act as a means to capture a man. When a woman uses sex as a cage, she is trapped with the man. Women don't realize they have given him the key and men will consume sex and her other gifts – the intangibles—with the same disregard.

Conditioning Children for the Yoke

As a community, we must protect our children from ingesting these lies about who they are. Our daughters are not safe if godly women remain silent and continue to allow this destruction. The next generations must not be allowed to be separated from their ability to express their wholeness and to fulfill the unimaginable plans God has for their lives.

Consider the dangers of early exposure to unharnessed sexuality.

If we expose our children to inappropriate sexual content at an early age, we engage something within them that is – made for a purpose – but for a later time in their lives. In fact, this early exposure to sexual content is sometimes called abuse.

> 24 Then God said, "Let the earth bring forth living creatures after their kind: cattle and creeping things and beasts of the earth after their kind"; and it was so. 25 God made the beasts of the earth after their kind, and the cattle after their kind, and everything that creeps on the ground after its kind; and God saw that it was good. (Gen 1:24–25, NASB)

Focusing a daughter's attention on pursuit of a man while she is still a child is conditioning her for the yoke of "the longing" judgment. But this is where many women have found themselves. By remaining enslaved to the longing themselves, generations of parents have ensured the following generations of young girls are prepared to be yoked by the judgment of longing for a man. Unfortunately, we have produced after our own kind.

Tuning them into "the longing" and encouraging their desires for a man early in their lives hinders their journey to wholeness and fullness of their identity in Christ and their identity in the world. The Bible is not meant to keep you from pleasurable experiences but to keep you safe within pleasurable experiences.

A woman's sexual expression is a key to her soul; therefore, wisdom is vital when deciding who will gain entry. Because entry through the sexual gate exposes the vulnerable sides of many areas of a woman's character, God requires sex to remain inside marriage. God's loving intent is not to withhold this great gift from the freedom of expression but rather to keep it protected and safeguarded in marriage so as not to imprison women or their feminine potential.

Think on this analogy: We do not teach our children to play in a busy street. We teach them how to play in the yard and not to stray beyond the sidewalk. To avoid the danger of the busy street, we take them to a park to play. We even teach them how to cross the street to avoid danger.

Some of the current proponents of unbidden sexuality say, "Kids are going to have sex anyway." But we never use this logic for acts that we see as dangerous. We never say, "Kids are going to drive anyway," and hand the keys to a five-year-old. We don't say, "Kids are going to go to first grade anyway," and push our two-year-old onto a school bus.

There is a right place for kids to do certain things. For driving, it is usually sixteen. For first grade, it is usually six. For playing in a busy street, it is *never*. In the same way, there is a right time and place to enjoy sex.

For a woman, the right place and the safe space to enjoy sex is in marriage.

God doesn't forbid sex outside of marriage to deny us pleasure. God forbids sex outside of marriage to protect us from pain. Access to sex, the passion and pleasure of this creative, exhausting phenomenon is the reward for committing the rest of your life to another person.

Wholeness

If we taught our daughters that they are whole and complete without a man, how would their lives be different? How would our lives, as women, be different if we believed we are complete without a man?

When contemplating wholeness from God's perspective, what could that mean? Are God, Jesus and the Holy Spirit one? Are God, Jesus and the Holy Spirit three individuals? They are three yet one. Are any of them incomplete without any of the others? Is the reality of the completeness of each member of the Trinity true? Of course! And we are made in His image. This is not a discussion of the validity of the Trinity. It is a challenge for you to think about your concept of being whole and a part of or intertwined with another.

In God's perfect creation of Eden, is it reasonable to conclude that God would create Adam as a complete being? Having an understanding of our God and His extravagance, as well as how He continually presents us with an abundance of gifts, wonder and splendor, can you believe He created Woman as less than complete and whole?

With this thought usually comes the protest that Adam and Woman made each other whole. Why would God create Woman if Adam was whole and needed nothing?

The question assumes that God only creates out of lack but Christians believe the opposite is true. We know that God creates in excess.

If we believed that God was a minimalist, meaning, He only created the necessities for life, what is our explanation for the millions of stars, galaxies and the expanse of the universe? Why would He create land and sea? Why not land or sea? Our Father is extravagant. In undefiled creation, He provided more than enough.

Instead imagine our God in His incomparable wisdom and love creating Adam to be fully satisfied in his environment, seeing nothing distasteful and finding pleasure in his life of discovering God's creation, dominion over the animals, while simultaneously appreciating their capacity and function in his world. In the same way, women are not empty shells only filled by a man's acceptance. Women are God-filled with infinite possibilities to affect their world.

The cultures of the modern world now give space for women to begin pouring their talents into their family at a later age. Women today feel a tinge of sadness when hearing of young girls marrying before entering their twenties. Women should be encouraged to exploit this time and treasure it not as a time of waiting for it to pass so they can enter completeness once coupled with a man. Women should discover and develop these talents in themselves for themselves and the community to which God has called them. This is the perfect time to spend with God as though there will never be another. This is the time to return to the garden and rejoice in true satisfaction with God until or if He decides to introduce you to your own Adam.

This space now given to girls and women is the perfect incubator for discovery, expression, and mastery of those womanly talents God gave us in the beginning. This is our chance to mature and celebrate our wholeness, to ignite the fires that God wants us to use to warm the world. This period of singleness allows complete focus on God, His love for us and discovery of His plan for us to impact our world.

And we have an enemy who has directed his hatred and energy devising and executing his plans to derail us from God's plan for our lives. This is the reason we have to know and wield the power of who God created women to be. Be careful to evade this pervasive trap described in these next few paragraphs.

Have you ever seen a flower on the brink of blooming? If you are a lover of roses in all their Southern glory, you will relate to this imagery. As the buds get bigger and begin to unfold, the gift of the delicate, fullness of the beauty that is a richly colored and fragrant rose proclaims that it is well worth the wait.

Have you ever been entranced by a play, a movie or a dancer's performance? Have you, in the enjoyment of the moment, found yourself completely immersed in whatever it was that captivated you?

Now, imagine the you are the owner of this treasure that has the ability to capture your heart, but it has also captured the attention of others. Imagine you had not had a chance to recognize the value of this treasure that you alone held. Even worse, imagine that the ones who wished to possess your treasure spent years perfecting a message for your consumption. These deceivers invested decades and careers and built industries implementing the method to convince you that your treasure, the gateway to your soul, had only the value ascribed by you, the one who had been deceived.

The sexual experience between a man and a woman triggers a feeling of oneness *for her*. This feeling permeates her entirely. It is why there are songs about satisfying sex causing women to stay with men who behave badly. It is why TV storylines are written about men with goals of casual sex who want to avoid female virgins. These women are too clingy, the plots say. This clinginess, that some despise, is the God-borne binding of her soul to his but, sharing sexual favors is not the same as being one with your husband.

Women, think deeply about the following questions. Experience your answers in light of what you have learned in this chapter.

With your first sexual experience, did you feel a bonding to that man?

How long did the feeling of being one with him last?

Did an incident cause the feeling to end?

What feelings do you attribute to that initial sexual experiences?

What was different about your next sexual experience?

If you could change your first sexual experience by removing it, delaying it, having a different partner, or any other scenario, would you?

Why?

Why does God keep sex encapsulated in marriage?

Understanding how God intended for us to connect spiritually and physically is important in understanding the reasons God has given us certain protective constraints on our behaviors. If we value our wholeness as women and desire to retain it unassaulted and unfractured, we must recognize the cost is to delay sexual activity until marriage. The payoff is that the door to distraction remains securely fastened, allowing us to remain focused and hone and grow our skills and talents as women.

This physical obedience to protect the spiritual self provides enormous dividends of pleasure in marriage. When the uncalloused soul of a woman can join, unrestrained, to the soul of her husband, God's will for pleasure and satisfaction finds a place to run wild.

You have made my heart beat faster, my
sister, my bride; You have made my heart beat

faster with a single glance of your eyes, With a single strand of your necklace. How beautiful is your love, my sister, my bride! How much better is your love than wine, And the fragrance of your oils Than all kinds of spices! (Songs 4:9–10, NASB)

May he kiss me with the kisses of his mouth! For your love is better than wine. (Songs 1:2, NASB)

This is the life God created and intended—purpose and pleasure.

But so many women have already forsaken the path of protection and have paid or are paying a debt because they believed the lie. The deceiver scammed us and we released our vulnerability to more than one man. By these decisions, women availed themselves to injury.

Let's discuss how these multiple strands of entanglement have left a trail strewn with the souls of those whose wholeness was murdered at conception. The wholeness of their souls was groped and molested as they staggered toward maturity as women.

God's love for women has always been for their best …

Chapter 8

Back to Adam:
From the New Birth Until Now

As Christian women, we have failed to realize that we are no longer under the judgment. We are no longer Eve. We must believe this and work toward a restored identity.

Through Jesus' death and resurrection, those who believe in Jesus are restored to their pre-fall nature. Their father is no longer the devil; rather, we are hidden in Christ and are new creatures.

Christian women must appropriate their restored identity as the daughters of God.

Now that restoration has taken place, the command, as an equal part of humanity, is to resume dominion on earth.

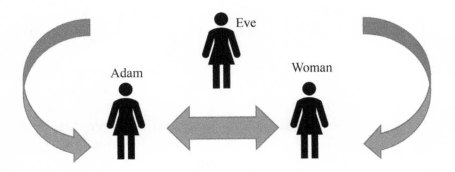

God's work of restoration through the death and resurrection of Jesus

Eve

Adam

Woman

If you are a Christian woman and have not been introduced to your Adam, you are Adam. As a Christian woman, if you are married, you are Woman.

Think about the characteristics of the female Adam. Before she met Adam, it was just God and *her*. In the place where it was the Father and the female Adam, she gloried in her Creator, her Father. How do I know? Because she was His creation and all creation worshiped God. During the time of just the two of them, she discovered her gifts and talents. As we have discussed, she wielded an intellectual perception that could see past the superficial aspects and peer into the deep things. This is the life of the perfected female Adam. This is what we should aspire to obtain for all single women—to be free from the judgment. Her longings should not be for man but for God.

God, You are my God; I eagerly seek You. I thirst for You; my body faints for You in a land that is dry, desolate, and without water. 2 So I gaze on You in the sanctuary to see Your strength and Your glory. 3 My lips will glorify You because Your faithful love is better than life. 4 So I will praise You as long as I live; at Your name, I will lift up my hands. 5 You satisfy me as with rich

food, my mouth will praise You with joyful lips.
(Ps 63:1–5)

As Adam was given charge to cultivate Eden, Woman was charged to cultivate connection: husbands, sons, daughters, family and community.

You may be momentarily disappointed because it seems women are, once again, being relegated to a subordinate place when paired with man. You are not! I challenge you to look at the skills and calling of women and then search any aspect of human life that should not be rightly impacted and transformed by what women are called to affect. They can transform humanity whether single or married. Women were created to execute change in humanity in any stage of life.

From the moment the first woman was introduced to her man, she was to protect him and be his ally. Whereas Adam could live as an island, Woman was the bridge to the mainland.

Equality

Equality is proclaimed repeatedly in Scripture. Because this topic is covered throughout our various discussions, I will not belabor the point. Be mindful of these familiar Scriptures if you ever begin to doubt who you are created to be.

> for there is no distinction between Jew and Greek, since the same Lord of all is rich to all who call on Him. (Rom 10:12, HCSB)
>
> He created them male and female. When they were created, He blessed them and called them human. (Gen 5:2, MT)
>
> 28 There is no Jew or Greek, slave or free, male or female; for you are all one in Christ Jesus. (Gal 3:28, HCSB)

When reading Galatians 3:28, notice after all subcategories of humanity are discarded: Jew, Greek, slave, free, male, female. We are told "all are one." This means all are equal. All are united in Christ.

Chivalry

If women believed they are equal, offense toward displays of chivalry would not be a familiar occurrence.

Chivalry is the traditional behavior of a gentleman. Today, some are pleased to think that chivalry is dead. Western culture used to require chivalry of men, especially toward a woman with whom they hoped to develop a romantic relationship.

Here are a few examples of behavior that was deemed chivalrous:

- Opening the door for a woman
- Walking on the street side of a sidewalk when with a woman
- Climbing the staircase behind a woman and going down a staircase in front of her
- Walking behind the woman you are with when being seated by a waiter or maître d'
- Walking in front of the woman when a path needs to be created through a crowd

Even reading these examples of chivalry, something deep inside a woman begins to stand up and say, "Yes, please. I would like that." These acts of male deference bring a smile to a woman's heart.

Chivalry is an outward acknowledgement of a woman's uniqueness.

Equal versus Identical

As a college student, I was taught that, because of my equality with men, I should not allow a man to open a door for me. To do so was to agree with him that I, a woman, was less than or weaker than him. At the time, I wholeheartedly agreed with what was being taught.

I gave a slightly disdainful expression to any lad who dared to hold a door open for me. But is this a rational reaction to such behavior?

Part of the issue is how we have come to describe equality. Equality, meaning we are valid and balanced contributors to humanity, has evolved to imply sameness to the detriment of women. Frankly, men and women are not identical.

In learning about God through the Bible—God's love written for us—without a doubt, God created us equal, but he did not create us identical.

From the beginning, man and woman were given gifts and purpose. Both the gifts and the purpose were complementary. Woman is literally created as an *ezer kenegdo*, which means "functional opposite."

Women must believe, they are equal and yet not the same as men. This thought is critical to our well-being and wholeness as daughters of God.

We must trust that our Father's love and integrity to know that He did not create a fractured human to bear the gift of dominion but instead created women whole and fully capable of absorbing and administering the responsibility of dominion. We must know whom God created us to be as equal dominators of the earth.

If we understood, deep within ourselves, how God created women, offense would not arise simply because a man opened a door or showed deference to a woman's femininity, her difference.

Consider this: When a young person gives up his seat for an elderly person, should the elder take offense? Would this act be rightly construed as a subtle smear, a decree of the elder's inferiority, or would it be more reasonable to understand the unsaid acknowledgement of respect for the elder's life experience and contribution to society? When a child forfeits his or her seat, it is a public recognition of the respect due to one who has existed in this world for a longer time.

Perhaps the child was prodded by a parent to forego the seat for the elderly person. Even so, it is the act itself, rather than the heart of the actor, that confesses a place of honor for the recipient.

In the same way, the man who opens the door for a woman *could* be misguided and believe that he is a more relevant being than the one he is serving; however, as she walks through the open door, his action and her heart agreeing with her place of honor.

God does not lie. Women are not identical to men. Women are equal.

Obedience and Submission: Which Is It?

I think it is safe to say we recognize what is means to disobey or not submit as when a request or demand is made, it is not acted on.

To ensure we have the same understanding of obedience and submission and disobedience and non-submission, I have provided a simple chart. I have given a scenario and a response. The answers are indicated in the table. Item 4 has been left blank to allow you to record your response.

	Scenario	Obey/Submit	Disobey/ Not Submit
1	The alarm goes off at five o'clock in the morning, your regular time to start your preparation for a work day. Your response: You open your eyes slowly and turn off the alarm and get out of bed.	✔	
2	While having breakfast with your spouse, your spouse reminds you that this week is your turn to clear the dishes from the table. Your response: After finishing your breakfast, you leave the house for an early meeting at the office without clearing the dishes.		✔

3	Driving to work, you get caught in a traffic jam. It delays your commute by twenty minutes. You are less than one block from your office and the light turns red just as you approach. Your response: You push down on the accelerator, but at the last second, you hit the brakes and come to a sudden stop.	✔	
4	Once at work, your manager informs you of the latest corporate policy. All essential employees must live within a five-mile radius of the company headquarters. You are an essential employee. You live eight miles away from the company headquarters. Your response: You explain to your manager you cannot sell your home and move within five miles of the headquarters.		

The chart identifies the difference between complying or not complying with a request. It also shows the outcome of compliance to a request is identical. You cannot tell if a person has submitted or obeyed by looking only at the outcome.

Before we address what is means to obey or submit, we need to ask ourselves if we truly understand the definition of these words. Are these words equivalent? Are they different, and if different, how so?

Let's try this exercise to determine if we understand submission and obedience. I will give you a scenario and a response. You must determine if the response is an example of obedience or submission. Indicate your answer by placing a check mark in the appropriate column in the table.

The first one is done for you.

	Scenario	Obedience	Submission
1	The alarm goes off at five o'clock in the morning, your regular time to start your preparation for a work day. Your response: You open your eyes slowly and turn off the alarm and get out of bed.	✔	
2	While having breakfast with your spouse, your spouse reminds you that this week is your turn to clear the dishes from the table. Your response: After finishing your breakfast, you remember a day from last week when your spouse did not clear the dishes. You keep your word and clear the dishes from the table.		
3	Driving to work, you get caught in a traffic jam. It delays your commute by twenty minutes. You are less than one block from your office and the light turns red just as you approach. Your response: You push down on the accelerator. You want to arrive promptly to the office but you think about the risk of a traffic accident by disobeying the traffic signal and the fact that disregarding a traffic signal is illegal. You engage the brakes and come to a sudden stop.		

4	Once at work, your manager informs you of the latest corporate policy. All essential employees must live within a five-mile radius of the company headquarters. You are an essential employee. You live eight miles away from the company headquarters. Your response: You tell your manager that you will have to return to her with a response. You plan to discuss this with your spouse once you return home. After an hour, you return to your manager's office and inform her you have decided to move.		
5	Your spouse returns home looking as if they had a stressful day at the office. After being home about an hour, your spouse announces a new corporate policy where all essential employees must live within a five-mile radius of the company headquarters. You live eight miles from your spouse's company headquarters. Your spouse tells you an agreement has been reached with headquarters. The family will move to comply with the policy. Your response: After asking several questions, you spend time thinking about the impact of moving. The next morning, you begin planning best preparations to sell the house and move the family.		

6	You are at midweek service at your church. The worship leader is on stage singing. He says, "Lift your hands and worship the Lord." Your response: You lift your hands.		

Responses are:

1. Obedience. To hear the alarm and adjust your actions to the expectation. No contemplation is involved. This is blind obedience.
2. Obedience. The act of clearing the table is obedience; however, in this scenario, your spouse reminds you of a previous conversation. It is likely that the conversation involved elements of negotiation when one or both of you submitted to the other to reach agreement.
3. Submission. Observing traffic laws should always be acts obedience. In the scenario presented here, there was not an automatic acquiescence to the traffic signal. The driver thought about the increased risk of causing or being a part of a collision and the ethical implication of breaking the law. Ultimately, the driver submitted.
4. Submission. Your listening to the new corporate policy, taking in the new information, and deciding to comply is submission.
5. Submission. Your requesting information to understand the rationale and implications of the decision before agreeing is the process of submission.
6. Obedience. Immediately raising your hands is obedience.

I hope the exercise helps to clarify the difference between submission and obedience.

Whether you obey or submit, the outcomes are the same. It is the process to arrive at the outcome that differs. Obedience does not question the demand. Submission must question the demand.

Obedience

The New Testament was written in Greek. Given that we are new covenant believers, review the Greek words for obedience ὑπακούω(hüp-ä-kü›-ō) **and submission** ὑποτάσσω(hü-po-tä›s-sō).

See this clearly. The words for obedience and submission are different. God's word has no confusion when these words are used. It is our misinterpretation of the definitions that has misconstrued what these words actually mean.

Using the HCSB, the verses containing the word for obedience are listed here. Read through them and think about who is expected to obey.

> Children, obey your parents in everything, for this pleases the Lord. (Col 3:20)
> But the men marvelled, saying, "What manner of man is this, that even the winds and the sea obey him." (Matt 8:27)
> And they were all amazed, insomuch that they questioned among themselves, saying, "What thing is this? what new doctrine is this? for with authority commandeth he even the unclean spirits, and they do obey him." (Mk 1:27)
> And they feared exceedingly, and said one to another, "What manner of man is this, that even the wind and the sea obey him?" (Mk 4:41)
> And he said unto them, "Where is your faith?" And they being afraid wondered, saying one to another, "What manner of man is this! For he commandeth even the winds and water, and they obey him." (Lk 8:25)
> And the Lord said, "If ye had faith as a grain of mustard seed, ye might say unto this sycamine tree, Be thou plucked up by the root, and be thou

planted in the sea; and it should obey you." (Lk 17:6)

And the word of God increased; and the number of the disciples multiplied in Jerusalem greatly; and a great company of the priests were obedient to the faith. (Acts 6:7)

And as Peter knocked at the door of the gate, a damsel came to hearken, named Rhoda. (Acts 12:13)

Let not sin therefore reign in your mortal body, that ye should obey it in the lusts thereof. (Rom 6:12)

Know ye not, that to whom ye yield yourselves servants to obey, his servants ye are to whom ye obey; whether of sin unto death, or of obedience unto righteousness? (Rom 6:16)

But God be thanked, that ye were the servants of sin, but ye have obeyed from the heart that form of doctrine which was delivered you. (Rom 6:17)

But they have not all obeyed the gospel. For Esaias saith, "Lord, who hath believed our report?" (Rom 10:16)

Children, obey your parents in the Lord: for this is right. (Eph 6:1)

Servants, be obedient to them that are your masters according to the flesh, with fear and trembling, in singleness of your heart, as unto Christ. (Eph 6:5)

Wherefore, my beloved, as ye have always obeyed, not as in my presence only, but now much more in my absence, work out your own salvation with fear and trembling. (Phil 2:12)

Children, obey your parents in all things: for this is well pleasing unto the Lord. (Col 3:20)

> Servants, obey in all things your masters according to the flesh; not with eyeservice, as menpleasers; but in singleness of heart, fearing God. (Col 3:22)
>
> In flaming fire taking vengeance on them that know not God, and that obey not the gospel of our Lord Jesus Christ: (2 Thess 1:8)
>
> And if any man obey not our word by this epistle, note that man, and have no company with him, that he may be ashamed. (2 Thess 3:14)
>
> And being made perfect, he became the author of eternal salvation unto all them that obey him. (Heb 5:9)
>
> By faith Abraham, when he was called to go out into a place which he should after receive for an inheritance, obeyed; and he went out, not knowing whither he went. (Heb 11:8)
>
> Even as Sara obeyed Abraham, calling him lord: whose daughters ye are, as long as ye do well, and are not afraid with any amazement. (1 Pet 3:6)

Looking at obedience, you may notice that, in the twenty-three times it is used in the New Testament, eleven times it refers to objects or entities that have no capacity to resist: e.g., the sea, the wind, servants, children, and demons.

Then there are many cases where obedience is expected from humanity, but the context presumes submission has already taken place: e.g., Abraham obeyed, those who accepted salvation obeyed, priests obeyed, and so on.

Obedience disregards your will. There is no choice in obedience. Obedience is a requirement. Obedience is demanded.

We have even created wedding vows that include this prison of obedience to a husband:

Bride: I, _____, take thee, _____, to be my wedded husband, to have and to hold from this day forward, for better for worse, for richer for poorer, in sickness and in health, to love, cherish, and to obey, till death us do part, according to God's holy ordinance; and thereto I give thee my troth.

On the day a couple celebrates the bride's transition from Adam to Woman, our traditions have tried to bind her to the life of Eve.

Being mindful of the definitions of "obedience" and "submission," a more meaningful relationship with both God and humankind can be expected.

A woman is called by God's word to submit to her husband. Just as humanity has innocently, and not so innocently, distorted the implementation of God's will in many other areas of life, we have succeeded in distorting this area too.

Over the centuries, the implementation of submission has mutated into obedience, servitude and sometimes, for all practical purposes, enslavement. This perverted and deformed picture of "submission" has made many healthy and whole women withdraw.

This fallen and wicked "submission" has caused our Christian culture to force women into a mold that God did not create. For those women who refuse to live inside this perverted mold, our churches have branded them with scarlet letters of "rebellious," "selfish," "difficult" and worse.

This bondage masquerading as submission steals a woman's true identity. It seriously wounds a woman's sense of her value and pushes her out of balance between thoughts and feelings into emotionalism. This "submission" destroys pieces of the daughter of God and insists that she is being obstinate when she refuses to stay silent during the amputation of her gifts and talents.

As humans, we tend to think more is better. Be cautious in the careless application of this thought to all aspects of God's instructions. Sometimes we are instructed to go the extra mile but this is typically related to exemplifying Christlike behavior toward unbelievers. Other times we are pointed to a precise activity. Be careful to avoid mindless obedience in cases where you are called to thoughtfully submit. If God has instructed you to walk forward ten paces and stop but you insist walking forward eleven or twelve paces will be even better, be warned, there could be a cliff at eleven paces.

> The fear of the Lord is the beginning of knowledge; fools despise wisdom and discipline. (Prov 1:7, HCSB)

Rejoice, you are not called to obey your husband. You *are* called to submit. Again I say, rejoice!

Submission

Submission is generally well discussed and equally despised. "What is submission and how do I get rid of it?" That was a question asked by a close friend of mine during the course of writing this book.

Submission is a willing acceptance of authority. It can only be performed by a thinking individual. It cannot be blind but must always be the outcome of a conscious intention. If ever the request cannot be denied, then compliance is no longer submission but obedience. Submission is given.

In a fallen world, submission is necessary to maintain order. It is not a sign of worth but simply a structure to manage conflict. At times this is hard to see, given the horrid history of men's domination of women, but the Bible is clear and God is not the author of confusion.

If we consider submission in our everyday lives, we see that we submit daily. This submission does not negatively influence our sense of self or our self-worth. When accepting a new career opportunity, we submit to the corporate policy. We affirm this submission by signing documents that require our obedience. We submit to our home owner's association's (HOA) and our bank's lending terms. We submit to the rules of the barbershop and the department store (no shoes, no shirt, no service). There are websites that ask if we accept or decline their terms of service. We have to decide if we will comply or refuse. This is submission.

You may think the forms of submission I've described are actually forms of obedience. They are not. The result of the submission could look like obedience, and that has been the source of confusion. Submission is a series of decisions. One decides to submit. With each request, a decision is made to submit. We see this in the life of our Christ, Jesus.

Jesus accepted God's redemption plan and stripped Himself of His divine authority to become a man. While on earth, Jesus perpetually submitted to His Father's will: Jesus was baptized; led into the desert for testing; answered the tempter with the Word of God only; was scourged and crucified for our sins. At each timepoint, Jesus had to decide to submit His will to God's will and then to obey.

In contrast, submitting to your husband in one request does not mean you become a mindless robot for subsequent requests. It is your responsibility as a wife, as an equal spiritual entity, to judge each request and then to *decide* whether to submit according to God's word.

Again, God is not the author of confusion. He has been clear in His love and through His word written to us thousands of years ago.

Wives, submit to your husbands as to the Lord. 23 For the husband is head of the wife, just as Christ is the head of the church, His body, of which He is the Savior. 24 Now as the church submits to Christ, so also wives should submit to their husbands in everything. (Eph 5:22–24, BSB)

18 Wives, be submissive to your husbands, as is fitting in the Lord. (Col 3:18, HCSB)

In the same way, wives, submit yourselves to your own husbands so that, even if some disobey the Christian message, they may be won over without a message by the way their wives live 2 when they observe your pure, reverent lives.

3 Your beauty should not consist of outward things like elaborate hairstyles and the wearing of gold ornaments or fine clothes. 4 Instead, it should consist of what is inside the heart with the imperishable quality of a gentle and quiet spirit, which is very valuable in God's eyes. 5 For in the past, the holy women who put their hope in God also beautified themselves in this way, submitting to their own husbands, 6 just as Sarah obeyed Abraham, calling him lord. You have become her children when you do what is good and are not frightened by anything alarming. (1 Pet 3:1–6, HCSB)

To sum up, each one of you is to love his wife as himself, and the wife is to respect her husband. (Ephesians 5:33, HCSB)

Think about this, at one time, women were considered to be little more than property. Marriage to a woman could be valued by a number of goats, sheep or cattle. Her virginity could be challenged, and if she had no bloodstained linen from her wedding night, she could be killed at the door of her father's house. It was during this time that God inspired fishermen, doctors, tax collectors, and the like to write words that would defy the cultural norms of the time and insist that women could disregard the chains and inequities of the law. Women could come to God as well as any man. This is the Father's heart.

Because of the tenor of the culture, this redemption from the law was tempered or ignored when it pertained to women. In many instances, even today, some churches still teach submission as if it is the equivalent of obedience. This is why many mature mothers of the church, who have a rich relationship with Father God, have not even thought to bring the notion of equal dominion to the fore for contemplation. Unfortunately, sometimes subjugation of women is so engrained that it is not questioned.

But this is the power of God's love. God reaches for us through fallen messengers and deposits a trail of gems that we can follow to find truth.

God's unflinching love is calling us to learn the difference between obedience and submission. His powerful love is calling women to fulfill His purpose in the world. He asks women to submit according to His definition and according to His plan.

The most effective way to submit to a man righteously is for a woman to first learn to submit to the One who never fails, the Eternal One, who is Jesus.

Judgment Free

In Christianity, we have a concept called redemption. Redemption refers to the state we live in because Jesus, the Son of God, bore the cost of our sins by giving His immaculate mortal life to save our sin-corrupted spirits. His death and resurrection are the method used to fulfil the law and set us free from the law and its penalties.

> For sin will not rule over you, because you are not under law but under grace. (Rom 6:14, HCSB)
>
> Therefore, no condemnation now exists for those in Christ Jesus 2 because the Spirit's law of life in Christ Jesus has set you free from the law of sin and of death. 3 What the law could not do since it was limited by the flesh, God did. He condemned sin in the flesh by sending His own Son in flesh like ours under sin's domain, and as a sin offering, 4 in order that the law's requirement would be accomplished in us who do not walk according to the flesh but according to the Spirit. (Rom 8:1–4, HCSB)

Christ's redemption enabled humanity to return to their rightful spiritual state before the fall. He redeemed us. His work is finished. We are free.

But to see how to live judgment free—free from the law of sin and of death—we need to understand what laws women labored under. We have to know this so we can make sure not to incorporate *any* of the Old Testament law into our lives or to pass along this law to our daughters in Christ.

Consider yourself warned. These laws seem extreme and unfair using today's modern worldview. I cannot reckon all the reasoning behind these laws but only that, due to the hardness of the heart of man, many laws had to be enacted. Ultimately, they worked toward the preparation of God's redemption plan for all of us.

Read further to see what women have been redeemed from. The Scripture reference follows the statement of freedom.

*****

You have been redeemed. You do not have to accept being less than the sole focus of your husband's affections! God gave Adam only one woman and He called it "good." You are not to be one of many wives. You do not have to accept polygamy.

> 19 Lamech took two wives for himself, one named Adah and the other named Zillah. (Gen 4:19, HCSB)

You have been redeemed. You do not have to give your body to anyone outside of marriage simply because of another's will.

> Look, I've got two daughters who haven't had sexual relations with a man. I'll bring them out to you, and you can do whatever you want to them. However, don't do anything to these men, because they have come under the protection of my roof. (Gen 19:8, HCSB)

Next, God addresses a practice where families literally sold their children. The law required men to be free of this servitude in the seventh year; however, women in this same service were not set free. It was dangerous for a woman to be single.

Fear not, **you have been redeemed.** You do not have to be sold into bondage. Nor do you have to be kept in bondage.

> And if a man sells his daughter to be a maid-servant, she shall not go out as the menservants do. (Ex 21:7, HCSB)

You are redeemed. In Christ, you can detect the seducer's wiles by adhering to and only believing God's word. In the event you have already lost your way, you are not obligated to stay in relationship with such a man outside of marriage nor are you required to consent to be his wife.

> When a man seduces a virgin who was not promised in marriage, and he has sexual relations with her, he must certainly pay the bridal price for her to be his wife. (Ex 22:16, HCSB)

You are redeemed. Christ's blood of Jesus has been shed for you. Blood can no longer defile you or make you unclean. You are free to enter the presence of the holy one when you are menstruating or blood flows from your body for any other reason.

> When a woman gives birth and bears a male child, then she shall be unclean for seven days, as in the days of her menstruation she shall be unclean. 3 On the eighth day the flesh of his foreskin shall be circumcised. 4 Then she shall remain in the blood of her purification for thirty-three days; she shall not touch any consecrated thing, nor enter the sanctuary until the days of her purification are completed. 5 But if she

bears a female child, then she shall be unclean
for two weeks, as in her menstruation; and she
shall remain in the blood of her purification for
sixty-six days. (Lev 12:1–5, NASB)

18 If a man sleeps with a woman and has
an emission of semen, both of them are to bathe
with water, and they will remain unclean until
evening. (Lev 15:18, HCSB)

19 When a woman has a discharge, and
it consists of blood from her body, she will be
unclean because of her menstruation for seven
days. Everyone who touches her will be unclean
until evening. (Lev 15:19, HCSB)

24 If a man sleeps with her, and blood from
her menstruation gets on him, he will be unclean
for seven days, and every bed he lies on will
become unclean. (Lev 15:24, HCSB)

25 When a woman has a discharge of her
blood for many days, though it is not the time of
her menstruation, or if she has a discharge beyond
her period, she will be unclean all the days of her
unclean discharge, as she is during the days of her
menstruation. (Lev 15:25, HCSB)

You are redeemed. You are not ruled by your husband. You
are free from the law. You do not obey but rather submit to your
husband's wishes. He does not have the ability to override your vows
and pledges unless you provide him with that privilege. God does not
require this action from you.

3 When a woman in her father's house
during her youth makes a vow to the Lord or
puts herself under an obligation, 4 and her father
hears about her vow or the obligation she put
herself under, and he says nothing to her, all her
vows and every obligation she put herself under

are binding. 5 But if her father prohibits her on the day he hears about it, none of her vows and none of the obligations she put herself under are binding. The Lord will absolve her because her father has prohibited her.

6 If a woman marries while her vows or the rash commitment she herself made are binding, 7 and her husband hears about it and says nothing to her when he finds out, her vows are binding, and the obligations she put herself under are binding. 8 But if her husband prohibits her when he hears about it, he will cancel her vow that is binding or the rash commitment she herself made, and the Lord will forgive her.

9 Every vow a widow or divorced woman puts herself under is binding on her.

10 If a woman in her husband's house has made a vow or put herself under an obligation with an oath, 11 and her husband hears about it, says nothing to her, and does not prohibit her, all her vows are binding, and every obligation she put herself under is binding. 12 But if her husband cancels them on the day he hears about it, nothing that came from her lips, whether her vows or her obligation, is binding. Her husband has canceled them, and the Lord will absolve her. 13 Her husband may confirm or cancel any vow or any sworn obligation to deny herself. 14 If her husband says nothing at all to her from day to day, he confirms all her vows and obligations, which are binding. He has confirmed them because he said nothing to her when he heard about them. 15 But if he cancels them after he hears about them, he will be responsible for her commitment. (Num 30:3–15, HCSB)

You are redeemed. You can marry whomever you choose within the family of God. You are not bound to marry into one group of humanity. The only criterion is that you not be unequally yoked with an unbeliever in Christianity.

> 6 This is what the Lord has commanded concerning Zelophehad's daughters: They may marry anyone they like provided they marry within a clan of their ancestral tribe. 7 An inheritance belonging to the Israelites must not transfer from tribe to tribe, because each of the Israelites is to retain the inheritance of his ancestral tribe. 8 Any daughter who possesses an inheritance from an Israelite tribe must marry someone from the clan of her ancestral tribe, so that each of the Israelites will possess the inheritance of his fathers. (Num 36:6–8, HCSB)

You are redeemed. Your body or your virginity are not the measure of your worth. While it is God's best for you to remain chaste until marriage, if you have already given this gift to another, God does not love you less. He will simply heal you more.

> 13 If a man marries a woman, has sexual relations with her, and comes to hate her, 14 and accuses her of shameful conduct, and gives her a bad name, saying, "I married this woman and was intimate with her, but I didn't find any evidence of her virginity." (Deut 22: 13–14, HCSB)

You are redeemed. God does not require your life if you commit sin; however, you heap the consequences of your error on yourself.

> 22 If a man is discovered having sexual relations with another man's wife, both the man who had sex with the woman and the woman must

die. You must purge the evil from Israel. 23 If there is a young woman who is a virgin engaged to a man, and another man encounters her in the city and has sex with her, 24 you must take the two of them out to the gate of that city and stone them to death—the young woman because she did not cry out in the city and the man because he has violated his neighbor's fiancée. You must purge the evil from you. (Deut 22:22–24, HCSB)

You are redeemed. Your worth cannot be measured in shekels of silver or gold or any other precious thing. Your worth is determined by the fact that Jesus gave His life for yours and you are made in the God's image.

28 If a man encounters a young woman, a virgin who is not engaged, takes hold of her and rapes her, and they are discovered, 29 the man who raped her must give the young woman's father fifty silver shekels, and she must become his wife because he violated her. He cannot divorce her as long as he lives. (Deut, 22:28–29)

You have been redeemed. You may marry your first husband again ... but why would you?

If a man marries a woman, but she becomes displeasing to him because he finds something improper about her, he may write her a divorce certificate, hand it to her, and send her away from his house. 2 If after leaving his house she goes and becomes another man's wife, 3 and the second man hates her, writes her a divorce certificate, hands it to her, and sends her away from his house or if he dies, 4 the first husband who sent her away may not marry her again after she has been defiled, because that would be detestable to the Lord. You must not bring guilt on the land the Lord your God is giving you as an inheritance. (Deut 24:1–4, HCSB)

What does all this mean? It means that you agree with our Father, God, when you:

- ✓ want to be with one man, the same man, for the rest of your life,
- ✓ want that man to love you and only you with fervent affection and loyalty,
- ✓ want to choose whom you will love and whom you will give your body to in intimacy,
- ✓ think you should decide your career path,
- ✓ believe that, because of the shedding of Christ's Blood, blood flow of a monthly cycle or other cause no longer defiles women or the covenant
- ✓ make decisions based on what you believe to be truth and in line with God's will,
- ✓ accept the marriage proposal of a Christian man who has declared his love and devotion to you regardless of his race, ethnicity, and so on

You have been redeemed. Live like you believe it.

As a Christian woman, turn your face to God's presence rather than hiding from Him as He comes to commune with you in the cool of the day. Never again be the daughter of Eve. You were created to be the daughter of God.

Chapter 9

What if God Called Her Adam?

What If God Loved Us?

What if your life was a testament to your beliefs? What if a person could watch you for a day or a week or some other amount of time and know that you were a lover of Christ? Not because you told them that you are Christian but because being a Christian is *who* you are.

If you recall the beginning of this book, I included some questions for you to ask yourself. You considered them deeply and responded.

Now that we have wrestled with ideas and constructs and culture, we are concluding our thoughts about God, Adam, Woman, and Eve.

Let's review those questions:

1. What does being Christian look like in your life? What will be different from today?
2. How does the Bible affect your everyday life?

Think of God.

3. What is the first image that pops into your head?
4. Describe the characteristics of that image.

5. Is God angry with you?
6. Make a list of how God expresses His love for you in every-day life.
7. Do you believe the Bible is true?
8. What does God say about sex?
9. What does He say about sex inside marriage?
10. What does He say about sex outside marriage?
11. Why does He make a distinction?
12. Is the rule about sexual relationships the same for men and women?

Are your responses to these questions different from the responses you gave before learning the truths in this book? Do you see how much of your view of the Bible is shaped *outside* of the Bible?

Here are some final questions:

1. Are men and women the same
    a) Physically?
    b) Emotionally?
    c) Spiritually?
2. Do you believe God loves you?
3. Do you believe he loves you a lot?
4. Does your life reflect the responses given previously?

"What if?" is a question that we must not only ask ourselves but also challenge ourselves to live out.

I hope you now see that as a Christian woman, you are not bound to long for a man.

> For sin will not rule over you, because you are not under law but under grace. (Rom 6:14, HCSB)
>
> Therefore, no condemnation now exists for those in Christ Jesus, 2 because the Spirit's law of life in Christ Jesus has set you free from the law of sin and of death. 3 What the law could not

do since it was limited by the flesh, God did. He condemned sin in the flesh by sending His own Son in flesh like ours under sin's domain, and as a sin offering, 4 in order that the law's requirement would be accomplished in us who do not walk according to the flesh but according to the Spirit. (Rom 8:1–4, HCSB)

The Lord your God is in your midst, A victorious warrior. He will exult over you with joy, He will be quiet in His love, He will rejoice over you with shouts of joy. (Zeph 3:17, NASB)

As the Father has loved me, so have I loved you. Abide in my love. If you keep my commandments, you will abide in my love, just as I have kept my Father's commandments and abide in his love. These things I have spoken to you, that my joy may be in you, and that your joy may be full. This is my commandment, that you love one another as I have loved you. Greater love has no one than this, that someone lay down his life for his friends. You are my friends if you do what I command you. No longer do I call you servants, for the servant does not know what his master is doing; but I have called you friends, for all that I have heard from my Father I have made known to you. You did not choose me, but I chose you and appointed you that you should go and bear fruit and that your fruit should abide, so that whatever you ask the Father in my name, he may give it to you. These things I command you, so that you will love one another. (Jn 15:9–17, NASB)

But God, being rich in mercy, because of the great love with which he loved us, even when we were dead in our trespasses, made us alive together with Christ—by grace you have been saved. (Eph 2:4–5, NASB)

But You, Lord, are a compassionate and gracious God, slow to anger and rich in faithful love and truth. (Ps 86:15, HCSB)

Give thanks to the Lord, for He is good; His faithful love endures forever. (1 Chron 16:34, HCSB)

"For the mountains may be removed and the hills may shake, But My lovingkindness will not be removed from you, And My covenant of peace will not be shaken," says the Lord who has compassion on you. (Is 54:10, NASB)

In conclusion, let's join the redeemed Chavvah, Eve, to imagine her life as Adam.

What If?

Walking into her loft apartment, Chavvah smiled dreamily and hummed a contented tune.

She turned slightly to close and lock the door, a smile still illuminating her face as she moved farther into the apartment.

"Today was a good day," she mused, catching a glimpse of herself in the mirror. She was curvy in a full and good way.

She began her day by meeting with friends for breakfast, then dashing home to take care of her to-do list with a bit of relaxation (a nap) mixed in. When she woke up, she dressed herself for a night of pampering from one of her suitors. She had enjoyed his conversation and company again. This was their third date.

Chavvah enjoyed this man because he was clearly attracted to her, but he also found his way into her ideas. Although he didn't understand a lot of her interests, he did understand that *she* had interests of her own and he didn't try to make them smaller than his own God-driven goals.

He was intriguing, a bit shy and he respected her thoughts. Unlike the guy from the previous week. Hmmm … his name slipped her mind. That guy was undressing her with his eyes from the moment she stepped from her car.

It always felt good to be wanted but she knew that no matter what he said, he couldn't see past her body and God's word warned that a relationship based on his lust wouldn't last and would only leave a scar for Him to mend.

Yes, that guy … what was his name? She really couldn't remember. He wanted her body, but she knew she was greater.

By his actions, he was willing to put his interests above hers. She turned her thoughts away from him glad she hadn't wasted brain space on his name.

She half closed her eyes slowly and sighing, plopped onto the sofa and let the cushions flop all around her. Instantly she regretted it since, as soon as her bottom hit the pillows, she thought it would be nice to have a cup of hot water with lemon to ease her digestion of

the memorable dinner. It was too late to ingest caffeine so her typical tea would have to wait until morning.

She'd eaten more than she should have at dinner but less than her taste buds craved. The food was magnificent!

She glanced at the sparkling skyline of the darkened city and its twinkling lights.

Then gathering herself up and freeing herself from the cushions, she shuffled into the bedroom and, in minutes, transformed from fancy to comfy. The beauty of living on the thirty-second floor was that there were no nosy neighbors to catch her walking around the house in her PJs.

Gliding into the kitchen, she filled a coffee mug with water and popped it into the microwave for three minutes.

While the water was heating, she took a lemon from the fridge and rolled it on the counter using the heel and palm of her hand. Once the lemon was fairly soft to the touch through the peel, she used a knife to slice the lemon across the middle, leaving two halves, each with a knotted end.

This was the time she wanted to spend with Jesus, this peaceful time between ending her day and falling into a fitful sleep.

"Jesus," she began, interrupted by the tone from the microwave to announce that it had finished its work. She opened the microwave door and grabbed the handle of the mug, which was now filled with steamy goodness.

Setting the mug on the counter, she started again. "Jesus, I love you more than I have ever imagined."

Contentment filled the silence.

She picked up one half of the lemon and squeezed it until juice flowed into the steamy water.

Chavvah stirred the water with a teaspoon and sucked the remaining juice and exposed pulp from the collapsed lemon. Then she tossed the remains of the lemon into the garbage disposal.

Closing her eyes, she lifted the cup to her lips and inhaled the tangy steam. "Thank you for this good day. Your gifts are beyond expression."

She sipped of the concoction on her way back to the sofa. Then she sat down carefully with the heated drink in her hands. Once again, the cushions greeted her, and she nestled her back into their comfort.

"What do you think of him?" She laughed. "I really think I like him."

She closed her eyes again and she listened and prayed. "Lord, not my will but your will be done." She meant it and her heart responded to the presence of the Lord rather than the tug toward the man.

Her mind moved on to her plans for the following day. She sipped a bit more "tea."

Remembering the handsy guy her best friend had set her up with two months ago, she shook her head. He said all the right things, but her spirit was disturbed by the way he touched her as though he was already her man. He wasn't as obvious as the man whose name still escaped her. This one was a bit more sophisticated. He knew he had what many women wanted.

Although many of her friends were settling just to have a man, she had shed that judgment long ago. She knew enough of the Bible to know that she was a treasure that this man, any man desiring her affection, needed to put forth an effort to attain it.

"Like the parable of a treasure hidden in a field," she said in a whispered.

No, this man had assumed that she would follow his lead simply because he tried to show her that she was worthy of his interest. What a waste of time!

Her eyes started getting heavy. She knew she would be asleep before midnight.

Putting her cup on the end table, she grabbed a pillow and stuffed it under her head. She pulled her legs in and told herself she would take a quick rest and then move to the bed. Without knowing it, she had lied.

The sun woke her up when its rays licked at the east wall, which was practically all glass.

She took a long time to stretch since the sofa was not the ideal place to sleep for the night after a long day, even if it had been a great day. Then she padded off to the powder room.

Coming from the bathroom, she tuned to her Pandora station, headed to her favorite chair by the wall of windows, picked up her journal and waited for the presence of the Lord to speak to her.

She heard the music, and her insides trembled with excitement and peace as His presence filled the room. Pen in hand, she started writing. She reached for her Bible and opened it to the Scriptures she had heard from His mouth.

As she read, she realized once again that her Father was a giver of good gifts. His love never fails. "He is relentless in His love for me," she whispered again only to herself.

She leaned back and let the Holy Spirit minister to her.

God had great plans for her. She loved it when He reminded her of who she was in His eyes. She was going to change the world. Again.

"Thank you, Father. Your love overwhelms me." With that Chavvah rested.

After a while, she rose from the chair refreshed and ready to accomplish all that the Lord had planned for her that day.

Her mind moved skillfully through the tasks ahead as she dressed. She stepped out of her bedroom and checked her reflection in the mirror. She lifted a few rebellious curls and used her fingers to ruffle her tresses for that trendy look. Then she turned and walked down the hallway to her front door. Opening it, she stepped out into the world.

Now!

After reading this book, I hope you see that as a Christian woman, you are not bound to the desire for a man. You are not bound to be ruled over or dominated by a man – any man - especially a husband who is your brother in Christ. As a Christian woman, you must turn your face to the presence of God rather than hiding from Him as He comes to commune with you in the cool of the day. Never again will you be the daughter of Eve. You were created to be the daughter of God.

You are her. How will you finish this story?

You are her. What does God want you to do for Him? Where does He want you to go? Who does He want you to meet? How does He intend to make it happen?

You are her. Allow God's Spirit to minister to you. Rise up refreshed. Get dressed and go out and conquer the world.

You are **Adam**: Live in wholeness as you submit to your loving Father's will.

You are **Woman**: Live in peace with who you are as a woman.

You are **Redeemed**: Live in power as Adam did in the beginning.

Live within God's best plan for your life. Walk powerfully in dominion as a daughter of God by returning to live in the place given to her, Adam.

About the Author

Emme Masters lives a quiet life with her husband in North Carolina. She has one son and a host of family members. She has a full-time career in clinical research and uses writing as a method of relaxation, expression and to document her walk with God.

Emme is a woman of strong, Christian faith. As a diligent study of God's Word, writing is her preferred vehicle to educate and intrigue readers.

You may also enjoy her first book now in the second edition: Crossing Over: Surviving the Chasm between Satisfied Single and Satisfied One

Emme Masters can be reached via email:

info@emmemasters.com
or
EmmeMasters@disciples.com

CPSIA information can be obtained
at www.ICGtesting.com
Printed in the USA
FSHW011111130319
56269FS